T0164968

Apprentice to Master

Katheryn Webb

Order this book online at www.trafford.com
or email orders@trafford.com

Most Trafford titles are also available at major online book retailers.

© Copyright 2010 Katheryn Webb.
All rights reserved. No part of this publication may be reproduced, stored
in a retrieval system, or transmitted, in any form or by any means, electronic,
mechanical, photocopying, recording, or otherwise, without
the written prior permission of the author.

Printed in Victoria, BC, Canada.

ISBN: 978-1-4269-2506-1 (sc)

*Our mission is to efficiently provide the world's finest, most comprehensive
book publishing service, enabling every author to experience success.
To find out how to publish your book, your way, and have it available
worldwide, visit us online at www.trafford.com*

Trafford rev. 1/13/2010

 www.trafford.com

North America & international
toll-free: 1 888 232 4444 (USA & Canada)
phone: 250 383 6864 ♦ fax: 812 355 4082

Mary Mills, My Mother for her early inspirition

Chapter 1

His mother called him Rob and sitting here alone on the river bank he thought about what she would say when learning he had just quit school. No matter what, he was determined never to go back. He watched the tadpoles and teased them with a stick as they swam around the rocks. It was early for tadpoles, but warmer than usual in Massachusetts, this spring day in May, 1910.

He threw his stick into the water, got up, and headed for home. His friends had already left school to help with the spring planting; they would return in the fall but he would never come back to this one room rural schoolhouse. All the whacks with a ruler across his back had marked more than just his body. He felt that his very being was in jepardy, and he would never allow his teacher to strike him again. The time had come for him to leave as planned on this his twelfth birthday.

He couldn't strike back but he could walk out and never come back; and that's what he did. After lunch and recess, he opened his desk top, picked up his slate and bookbag, walked past his teacher, past the potbelly stove, lifted his coat from its peg by the rear door and made an exit from this schoolhouse-box that had held him for six years. All the kids just looked at him, and the teacher shouted her last assault to his back as he threw the door open and slammed it behind him. He was gone--forever. He knew his mother would understand.

The age of twelve was important for any boy, but on this day it was especially so for Robert Webb, Jr. Not only was it his birthday but he had just made the biggest decision of his young life. From now on everything he did would be of his own choosing. With this one big decision, he knew his father would expect him to be totally responsible for himself. It was his mother however, who would confront him first. She spoke for his father and made the decisions, and the one immediate big concern was whether he could continue to live in the family home. He had made no plans for living anywhere else and hoped he might have a period of grace before leaving. He knew there would be little cause for celebrating his birthday at dinner tonight. His father was fearsome when he lost his temper, and Bob was prepared for the biggest whipping of his life. He knew his father would call him to the barn as soon as he found out what he had done.

By sheer bad luck it was his father he ran into first as he entered by the back garden, the shortest distance to the kitchen door. His father was plowing at the far end of the field and motioned Bobby to him. Caught, his defiance crumbled and his knees shook when his father demanded to know why he was home so early. He blurted out that he had quit school.

Robert Senior was so enraged he immediately dragged his son by his suspenders to the barn. His intention was to thrash him good but he realized that Rob had gotten too big to whip and instead he gave him a good tongue lashing. He told his son how, in England, he could never go to school and he had to learn figuring on his own and had not learned to read or write. Bobby had never heard his father speak so and he listened as the 'old man' went on to tell him how he, Bobby, had a chance his father had never had and how much easier it would have been for him if he could have had some schooling.

His speech aroused no flash of insight in the young man, as his father had hoped, and indeed it had little effect. Young Robert was not fazed. Out of words and expletives, and only an ounce of anger left Robert Senior picked up the nearby pitchfork--by way of making a final statement-- and threw it at his son, aiming to the side of him and at a bail of hay by the barn door.

Bobby, already half turning had taken a step toward the open door when the fork flew by. He turned and looked at his father; they allowed a split second to pass and then both broke out into laughter. Robert approached his son and put an arm around his shoulder saying, "I'm proud of you son. It's time you took a stand and left that old she-devil witch of a teacher. No man can let a woman beat on him that way." He then gave him a shove and pointing to the kitchen door said, "I don't know what we'er going to do with you, but I guess you must have some plans. Go talk to your mother." This only added to his anxiety and he felt little pleasure in getting the one thing he had wanted most from his father, acceptance of what he had done as well as confirmation that he was now a 'man'. He had no plans.

Bob met his mother in the kitchen where

she was measuring out flour. He always helped her bake bread and especially enjoyed pounding out the dough and rolling it into loaves. In the past year she had graduated him to being chief breadbaker and bought him his own separate stove so that they might not continually run into each other in the daily prepararion of large meals.

Breadbaking took time and required its own undisturbed space. Today, he stood before her earlier than usual-- although he might have stayed down by the river till school was out. She was aware of the time and knew something was wrong, but she could wait till he was ready to tell her. There was no use making up a story about it and, as he had boldly told his father, he came right out with it and told her everything. His mother listened and knew that she had heard it all before. She knew she couldn't talk him out of it and his decision this time was final.

She didn't blame him; he often came home with welts on his back, and more than once, she'd gone to the school and tried to solve the problem but the teacher was as stubborn as her son and there was no compromising. It seemed his teacher just wouldn't put up with Rob drawing in class, and he didn't plan to stop what he liked doing best. He was smart enough but would draw when he became bored. In addition he was skipping school more often than he was there. What point was there in his staying? There were no laws then requiring children to go to school.

Wiping her hands on her apron Mrs. Webb turned to her son and said, "Rob, you know your father won't let you live here without being in school or working. Your three older brothers do all the farm chores and he just doesn't have work for you." She was concerned for him, that he might end up working in the mills as so many children did who quit school before their teen years. As a teenage boy he would have a chance of becoming an apprentice with a tradesman. She had hoped he could have lasted until the eighth grade when most farm boys quit to begin their life's work.

Bob was in a bad spot, yet he knew what he wanted to do. Unrealistic as it might have seemed he wanted to be an artist, and in New England at that time, there were a number of successful artists. Mrs. Webb knew of several who lived in Massachusettes and were making a good living. She knew Robby had talent and the willpower to work hard. He had a right to his dream and she had faith he could succeed. She and his father had left England to come to America with their own dreams.

Chapter 2

Hannah, Bob's mother, had been "sold on the block" as a skivy maid to a wealthy family in England. They allowed her to mingle with their children and she learned to read and write along with them. She spent time at the stables and while learning to ride and care for horses, she also gained knowledge of thoroughbred racers. This would put her in good stead later in her new land and farm life, when her husband Robert, who had come to America with her, would allow her the hobby of training and racing a wellbred horse.

Hannah claimed that her father was a priest in the Anglican Church, assigned to Westminster Abbey! How these two events-of being a skivy maid and the daughter of an educated man of the cloth-could be reconciled is a mystery. Bob would tell the story repeatedly throughout his lifetime. His father confirmed it, stating that they were married by his wife's father in an alcove at Westminster Abbey. The priests were not permitted to marry anyone within the sanctuary as this was reserved for royalty. The bishop had given his permission for the marriage on the provision that it would not be written in the registry.

Times were very hard in late nineteenth century England when Robert James Webb came of age. The older people in various communities saved their small change and came together each month to buy two tickets on a ship to America. They wanted their children to have a better life than they had known, and the new world was their hope. The young people who wanted to go put their names in a hat for a drawing of just two names- a man and a woman.

Sometimes, the young man and woman didn't know each other, but were required to get married before they left. Robert James Webb did not know Hannah Maynard before they met at that drawing. He was thirteen years older than the young skivy maid seeking to better herself by placing her own name in the hat. This man who would be her husband was over six feet tall.

She was five foot two and still in her early teen years.

Robert and Hannah were married by her father as soon as cleared by the bishop of the Church of England and immediately boarded their ship for the new world. Their passage had been purchased but Robert was still required to work the bellows pump four hours on and four hours off, night and day, for the forty-two days it took to get to Boston. His young wife served round the clock as maid to first class passengers on board. The young couple saw each other only in passing, for the entire trip. It was a half-sail half-steam cargo ship that went to Scotland and around the tip of Africa before heading out across the Atlantic.

Before entering the harbor in Boston, the captain called a meeting of all the young people leaving England for good. The captain, like many people of station in England, didn't like losing their young people. If it were their old or disabled it would be different but to lose their youth ment to loose Englands future. For turning their backs on the mother country he would punish them. In order that they have no reminder of home, or England, just before the ship docked he had them gather up and throw overboard all their posessions. This was not hard for the Webb couple as they had very little. To comply they discarded their toothbrushes, combs, and even the pallets they slept on. All was thrown into the sea so that when they landed at Boston they had only the clothes they wore. They were met by English immigrants who welcomed them to the new world and helped them get established.

Robert Webb brought his skills as a brick mason and carpenter with him, and applied them to building a home for his growing family. Looking back over fifteen years, he was proud of his accomplishments. First he worked in a soap factory and saved everything he could until he had enough to buy some land. He purchased 150 acres with a little shack and horse stall on it and did farming. In time he was able to build other houses, besides his own, some of which he rented and some he sold.

His wife was an asset to him in that she could read and write and took care of the rentals. She was good at figures and knew what to charge. Her management skills carried over to the home and her place as mother. She put up with no nonsense from their five boys and one girl, but would listen to her children when they had needs that called for her wisdom. Rob needed her now and her husband knew she could handle his situation.

He knew she would speak for him, advising

the boy that he could not continue to live in the family home rent free and without responsibilities. He knew the boy was not lazy and would be responsible. Rob had made some mistakes; once when collecting the rent money, he had laid the leather purse, full of money, on a stone wall while he played ball. No one took the money, but he had to be corrected so as never to repeat such a thing again. And then, there was the time when he tragically caused his best friend a disabling injury. Robert Senior, in part, blamed himself for that. His son was performing a job he himself had assigned to him. Bob Junior was very young; and his father knew he should have taught him better how to use an axe. The accident had destroyed the boys' friendship and that between the two mothers. Robert Sr. felt that his fourth son, and namesake, had overcome this tragedy and, like himself, could be successful without a formal education.

Chapter 3

A glimpse into the future would see the young Robert Webb Jr. walking with the giants of American industry, entertainment, religion and art. They borrowed his talent to fulfill their own dreams and visions for America. All he wanted to do was paint, and he worked hard for the great men who commissioned him. He decorated the mansion of John and Mable Ringling, of circus fame. He recalled, in later years working for so many men at the same time, he didn't know who would be paying him at the end of the month! In the case of Mr. Rockefeller, he might work two different jobs in two different cities and be on different payrolls. While at Colonial Williamsburg in Virginia, Rockefeller would occasionally send his plane down to the small airport in Williamsburg to pick up Bob and bring him to New York or elsewhere to decorate a home, a church, library, or apartment building.

At the age of twelve, he had no clue about his future, of course. He only knew then what he wanted to do and, along with a natural talent, he had a capacity for hard work. His father was not insensative to his situation and knew that what he needed immediately was work. He and his wife, Hannah, could do what they had done for the three older boys; give them jobs on the farm and teach them what they knew until they could apprentice to some tradesman. Robert felt he could keep his namesake busy until he was thirteen and at that age he too could go out on his own and find an apprenticeship with a painter. He gave his son this year of grace.

With jobs his father gave him, and his mother using him to sell her eggs, run errands, and collect rents in town, Rob kept busy. Hannah had taught him to cook and bake, and with eight family members plus workers on the farm and at the building sites, he was the second set of hands she needed in the kitchen. The one daughter in the family was the oldest child and had already taken a job in town as a nurse. Bob became a good cook; a skill that launched him into the Navy later on, until he was assigned to his proper position as a camouflage artist. His cooking skill remained a lifelong pleasure to him.

Determined to be on his own as soon as possible Robert Jr. turned to an artist friend, Carl Melby whom he'd known for several years. Old Man Melby, as he was called, sat in a store front window and painted.   Shoppers would stop by and watch him with fascination. He was good. He placed a tin cup by the door and lookers on would drop coins in for the privelege of watching him. Bob first came to know him when collecting rents in town for his mother. On cold New England days, he'd stop by and press his nose to the glass watching until it nearly froze there. Bob was probably about eight when he first met Melby and he kept coming back when in town running errands; or when he skipped school to be there.

One day, Carl motioned him to come in. He had a cat he called Miss Meow. This was an unusual feline that did tricks and sat on Carl's shoulder while he painted. Bob was fascinated by both the painters skill and by his cat. The man and boy came to know and like each other.

Carl had other jobs he did for a living, and he began to ask the lad to go with him. These jobs were usually in barrooms, public buildings, and sometimes churches, where he would paint or restore decorations. He taught Bobby, as he called him, how to mix colors and keep track of what colors he put together to make new ones. He put them in pots with numbers so that when he was on a ladder, he would ask for a color by number and Bobby would lift it up to him.

His mother learned what he was doing when some of her friends observed him going into barrooms with 'old man Melby.' They reported it to her. She said she trusted her son and his friend whose wife she was acquainted with. Carls' wife had told her once that he could speak five languages and had traveled the world- the reason he had so many stories to tell Bobby. When others thought of him as eccentric, the youngster looked up to him as someone special.

Mrs Webb appreciated that the old artist was teaching her son how to do the things he wanted to learn, as the mixing of colors, drawing , and how to paint. She probably didn't know that the subject matter on bar mirrors was usually naked women reclining on velvet settees, but it wouldn't have mattered to her. For a woman of her time, she was broad-minded. For young Bobby it was occasionally embarrassing. One bartender had a pump rigged up under the counter. An air tube went from it to the painting of a female with exposed breasts. The breasts were made of balloons so that when inflated, or deflated, the breasts would rise and fall with the pumping of his foot! When a patron got too anebreated and it was time for him to go home the bartender would work his foot and cause him to think he was seeing things. He would leave in a hurry!

His father had heard Rob say wistfully that if he had a bicycle, he knew he could find delivery work. Rob knew he needed money for the bike and he needed the bike to make the money! He had been walking long distances carrying a basket with eggs and, on occasion, if the weather was too bad, his father had allowed him to take the mule. He hated that mule; it never did what he wanted it to do, or it would just stand and not move. Thus he learned why his mother sometimes said he was 'mule headed.' Robert Sr.didn't tell his son, but he had in mind looking around for a used bike for him the next time he went to town.

The barbershop in Metheun was the place to get information of all kinds. He could ask there if anybody knew were he might get a bike. It was time for his haircut anyway and upon entering the shop there were two men ahead of him and one in the barber chair. When they finished talking politics, he asked if anyone knew where he could pick up a used bicycle. They told him about a yard sale on Mystic Lake Road that had just started that day.

Deciding to come back later for his haircut, he unhitched his horse and small utility wagon, which he'd brought along to carry the feed and hay he needed to buy. With one easy stride he lifted his tall frame to the seat and gathered up the reins and with a "git" to his horse, he headed for Mystic Lake Road. It was a good sale and he regretted he hadn't known about it in time to bring Hannah along.   Perhaps he could find something to take home to her – a kitchen gadget, sewing needles, or whatever looked good. Something registered with him that this had been a special day for them but he couldn't decide what it was. It may have been when they first landed in America !

While he was walking and looking there was a bicycle with a "For Sale" sign right in front of him. The paint on it was dull, but it appeared to be sound. Before he could try it out, he asked the seller to adjust the seat for his height. He checked to see if the brakes worked and whether it rattled badly or not. One plus was that it had a large wire basket on the front over the wheel and attached to the handle bars. The basket was sturdy and deep and held by firm leather straps. He rode the bike around and it checked out all right. He wished, though, that Hannah was here because she was much better than he at bargaining for a good price. He told the seller he wasn't sure about it, and would send his son back to look at it himself. The seller didn't want him to leave without commiting to buying the bike; he was afraid of losing the sale. Robert realized that what he said sounded like bargaining with the man, though he had not intended to.

Since he'd started in a bargaining mode, he decided to take it to the next step by pointing out one or two minor defects he now noticed, such as worn handlebar grips and a scratch on the rear fender. Robert then offered the seller several dollars less than he'd asked. The seller shrugged his shoulders, sighed and said, "well, fine if you really want it, it's yours," as he extended his hand in the accepted language of the day to close a deal; it meant that an agreement had been reached. Robert was pleased, shook his hand, and fished out a sock in which he carried his money, untied the knot and counted out what the merchant had agreed to.

Deciding again not to get his haircut, he put the bike in the wagon, and went directly to the feed store where he bought hay and some oats for the horses, then headed home with the bike, thinking of how Bobbie could pay him back for it. He felt that something could be worked out whereby his son could pay him a portion of his earnings over a period of time. With the basket, Bob could make deliveries for local merchants, as well as carrying items for his mother.

There were other ways he could help his son earn money to work off his debt. He was building another rental house, and could use him as a 'handyman' or 'gofer,' meaning one who runs to fetch things for the workers. It was time he began to learn a skill that he could fall back on when his art work wasn't selling. Carpentry had been a good trade for the old man. His youngster just might take to it.

It was then he remembered that he had intended to get a gift for his wife at the yard sale. He didn't know why this date seemed important but felt he should remember. No doubt it was an anniversary that Hannah would remind him of. He had gotten distracted by buying the bicycle and turned the horse around and went back. This time, he hitched the horse and wagon where he could keep an eye on them and shopped only at the tables within sight. There was jewelry, kitchen cutlery, and a table of fancy ceramic vases. He liked these, and bought a pretty blue and green vase that Hannah could put on a window sill or display on the hutch he had made for her. He was pleased with himself and finally turned the horse homeward. His haircut could wait for another week.

On arriving home, he drove straight to the barn and unloaded the wagon, leaving the bicycle beside the horses' stall. He brought the vase into the house and put it on a shelf in the hutch. His wife was not in the kitchen, and his son was nowhere around. He went to the construction site of the new tenant house he was building, and did not come home until dinner time.

Chapter 4

When all were seated around the table, Hannah just kept looking at her husband with a radiant smile and knowing look. He had remembered their special day when they set sail for America from Dover, England. Then everyone noticed how Rob squirmed and lifted his fork in the air and finally said, "Oh, wow; where did that neat bike come from that's down in the barn?" His mother added quietly, "And that beautiful vase on the hutch ?"

Such display of generosity was out of character for Robert Senior, and he regretted he had done it. He feared they thought he was getting senile. It didn't take long, however, for appreciations to take over and plans made for young Robert to assume responsibility for helping to build the new tenant house under construction.

Hannah loved her husband for this rare show of thoughtfulness and especially for what he was doing for Robby. His violent anger in the barn when he learned Rob had quit school had frightened her, she could hear him all the way to the kitchen! However this time he had not put a hand on young Robert but rather shouted and vented a flurry of expletives his son had never heard before, she felt sure. The pitchfork had stopped them both in their tracks and the storm was over. Hannah was glad as she loved both of her men. Robby no longer felt guilty for what he had done and his father felt a pride in him for showing his starch by not taking any more injustice from his teacher. He was growing up and both his parents knew he would do all right in the world.

Robert Webb Senior had not rejected his namesake and would go on to help him until he reached more maturity. Rob, on the other hand would continue to respect his father, not out of fear but in a new, hardly understood, bond of a shared manhood. Bob had been initiated on his twelfth birthday and had passed a bigger test than he was fully aware of. Not to have finally taken a stand in his school situation and allowed one more beating might have ruined him. He did what he had to do and it launched his future.

Bob's first trip on his new bike was a delivery job for his mother. Before returning home, he stopped by to visit with Carl Melby and ask him about the upcoming art show at the museum in Boston. Carl wanted him to enter the show, and Bob wanted to know more about it.

There was an unwritten communication between artists in New England. They exchanged information of shows, visiting artists, jobs, and other news of interest to the art community. Bob's friend told him about the show sponsored by the Museum of Fine Arts in Boston. It was an open show in which any area artist could enter a painting that would be judged, and only the best works would be accepted for exhibition. Though the entry deadline was only three weeks away, Melby thought Bobby was a good enough painter to get into the show and he encouraged him to start painting right away. Bob couldn't wait to get started. His concern was whether there was enough time for an oil painting to get dry.

He usually did his art work in his bedroom but this time he chose as his place of work, near the kitchen window, where there was plenty of light all day. He asked his mother if he could invade her work place. The odor of oil paints mixed with cooking smells would be enough for her to say no, however she helped him get set up there. His sister Jane suggested he paint a vase of wildflowers. His mother contributed her lovely ceramic vase, and he picked a bunch of the prettiest flowers he could find in an adjacent field.

After about three days of painting, the bouquet began to wilt. Not wanting his painting to wilt with the changing flowers, he returned to the field and picked some more. There were so many varieties, it was hard to find ones that looked like the originals. At this early stage in his career as artist, he learned what has always been a problem for artists painting still lifes of flowers, fruits, dead birds or animals--that was in finding replacements to keep the painting looking fresh and the same while it was worked on.

To add life to their work some artists also had the skill to paint a fly or bee with transparent wings perched on a fruit or flower. He tried adding a bee but realized he didn't have time for the trial and error neccessary to make it look real. He didn't accept that he wasn't ready yet to take on such a challenge. For this painting, his problems with freshness, and change of light and shadows, were problem enough. The bee could wait.

Bobby knew, from what Melby had told him, that for those who had the resources, the problem of animal or bird replacements, when they got stale, was solved by using taxidermy objects as Audubon did. Bobby would not take up taxidermy work. Although he hunted with his father and brought home small game he never tried drawing from it--or embalming it! Anyway, that wouldn't help him now with wilting flowers. He knew of no way to preserve them and replacing was the only answer.

After a week, Bob felt that he had worked long and hard on the painting, and yet it had a spontaneous, fresh and colorful look. His mother, sister and brothers, who were his best critics, liked it. Notice of the show finally came in the newspaper, and Bob was glad to have the date of entry confirmed. He trusted old Melby's memory, but felt better knowing the date for sure. The next task was to make a frame for the painting. With the help of a simple mitre box, his father had made for him, he cut, nailed and glued together scraps of moulding , from the tenant house he was helping his father build. He then gave color to his new frame by thinning down an oil pigment to match a color in the painting, and he stained it.

His sister, Jane, begged to have the painting

after the show was over since the idea of wildflowers had been hers. He told her maybe so if he could sail with her boyfriend on his sloop "The Blue Goose." Her boyfriend was a champion sailor and was winning all his races. Bob was proud of his sister and her choice of boyfriends. Hero worship in the young at that time was for athletes, as it has been down through the ages. Jane was especially fond of her two youngest brothers, and they looked to her for help many times, especially for their sewing needs. She would try to work it out that he have a day of sailing. With a commitment that he would give her the painting after the show, she did just that.

One of Jane's favorite amusing stories was about the time when Bob and younger brother, Arthur, came to her asking if she would make bloomers for their pet runt pig! They had begged their father to give them the pig rather than dispose of it as was his plan. To feed it wasn't worthwhile as it would never have any value on the farm or at the market. He made them promise to feed it and take care of it. Winter was coming on, and their bedroom above the kitchen was very cold. They thought that if the pig could sleep with them they could stay warmer. Their mother would hear nothing of it unless the runt were outfitted with a diaper so as not to soil their bed.

Jane measured the pig and made a pattern. It was a kind of diaper made of sail cloth and fit very snuggly with rubber elastic sewn at the legs and around the waist. That first night, as expected, the runt did his business and in the morning, according to the plan he and his brother Arthur had made, Bob took his turn first for emptying the diaper. There had been a heavy snow during the night. Bob opened the window and took the pig by the legs and shook it vigorously. With it's squeallying and squirming, he lost his grip and it slipped from his hands, and out of it's bloomers, and dropped head first into the snowbank outside the kitchen window!

Mother Webb, at the sink, looked up just then to see a pink bottom sticking up out of the snow. She exclaimed, in alarm, "Oh, my poor Rob has fallen out of his window!" She rushed out to retrieve him from the snowbank only to discover it was the runt pig! That ended the boys experiment. No more pig. It probably ended up on some tenant family's dinner table.

Chapter 5

*B*ob was ready to deliver his painting to the museum, though it was barely dry. His mother decided to go with him. She knew he could go alone but she wanted to go into Boston for a little window shopping. When he was very young, she had often taken Rob to church with her in Boston at the Mary Baker Eddy's Christian Science Church. They would not be going there this day, however.

Methuen was a short distance from Boston, about fifteen miles, and the train pulled into the station just before noon. Mrs. Webb had brought some of the egg money along. This was hers; she kept it for special occasions, or emergencies, and this day she thought they would eat lunch in a restaurant near the museum. She knew Boston well, having come into town frequently, not only to attend the church but to other places, where séances were offered. This form of entertainment was very popular then. She'd brought Robby along to these, but he became restless and annoying to the assembly as any youngster would. A child wasn't interested, after all, in trying to raise the dead, none of whom he had ever known. She quit bringing him and went by herself. He would remember these occasions for a lifetime, recalling as a small boy being under the table and watching feet and hands manipulate the table so as to make it move and cause people to think spirits were doing it.

On this day Mother Webb found a little restaurant around the corner from the station, which had checkered tablecloths and waiters. It was clean, and she knew they would like the food. It was a treat for Bob, not only to eat lunch in a restaurant, but to have his mother all to himself for a change. After lunch, he watched her intently as she went over the bill carefully adding up the figures to see if they were correct before she paid the waiter. This was a learning experience for the youngster and one he would carry with him. He remained frugal but generous with his money all of his life.

Bob had been just as careful with his painting,

leaning it against the wall beside his chair. It was barely dry enough to handle. He wished he had learned of the show a little earlier. He told himself, however, that there was an advantage to having less time in that he had to work faster. His work looked more spontaneous and he knew that meant something to the judges. He also knew the colors could get muddy looking from being overworked.

Entering the museum, Bob felt as though they were walking on hallowed ground. For the first time, he was looking at some of the greatest paintings in the world by artists whose works he had only seen in print or books that Carl Melby had shown him. What a difference! These paintings were alive and vibrant with color; and he could see all the brush strokes. A thrill of excitement gave him goose bumps. He and his mother walked through the galleries, taking it all in and speaking only in a whisper. It was a religious experience.

A guard stopped them, wanting to know their purpose with the painting. Holding his painting by the wire on the back, Bob explained, and was directed to a downstairs room where others were dropping off their pictures. He left his painting with an individual who stuck a number on the back and gave him a receipt. On the way home, he walked in a kind of daze as his mother took her time looking in the shop windows. On the train, he was still off in another world, and to look at him his mother knew how much the trip had meant to him. She knew he had found his calling; he would go on to become an artist.

Each day, at home on the farm, he waited for the postman. Mr. Wiggins could be spotted some distance away by the government issued wagon and faithful border collie "Tippy" tagging along between the rear wheels, as was customary with border collies. Two weeks after their trip to Boston, Bob ran as he always did to the end of the lane and pulled out a long envelope from the box. The return address said, " Museum of Fine Arts, Boston." His heart pounded as he ran back to the house where his mother was waiting to read it. It read:

"Dear Mr. Robert Webb, Jr:

Your recent entry of an oil painting in the open show sponsored by the Museum of Fine Arts, Boston has been accepted for exhibition.

Congratulations !

You are invited to a Varnishing Party where the members of the museum and artists may meet and get to know each other. This is a black tie affair for prospective exhibitors.

Sincerely,
Director of the "Museum of Fine Arts, Boston"

Although proud to have been accepted for the show, Bob was alarmed about the varnishing party. He thought it meant that the paintings would all be varnished! This shouldn't be done to his work because it wasn't dry enough. He knew that an oil painting had to dry for at least a year before varnishing. Otherwise, the varnish, in drying faster than the paint, would shrink it causing cracks over the whole canvas. He would just have to go to the party to protect his work.

When the day of the party finally came, his mother had prepared Robs best Sunday clothing; as he had no formal clothes she thought these would do. She helped him tie his string tie, and gave him money to buy train tickets. Her last minute instructions were of how to behave properly and to say "please" and "thank you." He was to leave the party early enough to catch the train home. She forgot to warn him about what might be in the punch bowl, or that the ladle was not the same as the dipper that hung on their pump by the kitchen door !

This was one of fancy glass that glittered. It was awkward to handle when he tried to drink from it ! The hostess was very kind when she took it from him and handed him a glass cup. He thanked her and found the punch to be very pleasing. It warmed and tickled his insides as it went down. Indeed, he liked it so much he returned more than once for refills. By the time he boarded the train for home, he was walking a little sideways and giggling to himself. He was especially happy to learn that the party was social and "Varnishing" was only a name put to it.

He was aware that he was just a kid. No one let on, however, that he presented himself as a country bumpkin! Just the opposite; everyone took a liking for him and were facinated by stories he told of his life on the farm. People, in their formal attire had approached him, as he was different and very young to be entered as an artist in this show. He was enjoying himself and had already developed his storyteller style, laced with animated humor, thus drawing people around him. The punch bowl no doubt helped. He told them of the runt pig and the bloomers his mother required it to wear to their bed. He had everyone rolling in laughter. The country boy with a self-deprecating humor won the hearts of these art lovers.

Luckily, he had not visited the punch bowl too often when he decided to make the rounds of the show and see what others had painted. He found his own painting hanging beside another still life with more subtle colors than his own. This complemented his work and he was pleased. He turned a corner and before him was a large painting of a seated woman. He caught his breath and stood transfixed, staring at it. Someone behind him asked, "Do you know her?" Bob kept looking and replied, "Yes Sir," knowing he was addressing a gentleman, "she is Mrs. Eddy. Mrs. Mary Baker Eddy."

A tall, distinguished-looking gentleman with an elegant lady at his side stepped forth. He introduced himself as Fred Mortimer Lamb and wife. He was the artist of this portrait. Bob was awe struck as he knew him to be the best portrait painter in New England. Bob told him the likeness was perfect and he was honored to meet him, the painter. Lamb enquired as to how Bob knew Mrs. Eddy and Bob told him about his mother going to the Christian Science Church. He had often gone with her.

Mr Lamb said he had seen Bob's painting of flowers and was impressed with it. They found chairs and sat down for a while to talk and Bob told them of his troubles in school and how his father didn't have work for him on the farm. Mrs. Lamb took a liking for the young man and felt a motherly interest in his situation. Lamb had worked as an art teacher in the public schools and saw promise in young Bobby. He told Bob he would like to give him a few hours each day and could teach him both landscape and portrait painting. He would call it an apprenticeship but would not require any contract or fee for him to learn. Neither would he pay him anything for the small tasks required of a painter's apprentice.

Bob found that the apprentice tasks extended to splitting logs and stacking them for the Lamb's fireplace, and clearing brush on the property. He didn't mind as he always had more energy than he knew what to do with. He would be turning thirteen very soon and knew his father's commitment to him would be ending. He had told the Lambs this and didn't know why he had talked so much about himself. They had a kindly interest and were offering him an opportunity that may never come again. He wanted to take it.

Bobby went about finding his own place to live and an evening job to go to, in order to pay rent and buy food. The prospect of learning from Mr. Lamb was very exciting. He knew the merchants in town, having been delivery boy for some of them, and thought that if he could work as a stock boy at night and sleep in the store, he could study with Mr. Lamb in the daytime. And so he went to each of them seeking employment and lodging.

When he found a store whose merchant he knew and was interested in hiring him, he told his mother. She wanted to go with him and look over the living arrangments. He would have his own attic room above the store and his mother talked with the merchant and saw that Bobby would be earning a fair wage. She went with him as well to meet Mr. and Mrs. Lamb and learn of what plans they had for young Bobby to start his beginners learning to be a painter. Thus he began his apprenticeship with F.M. Lamb and earned enough as a stock boy to take care of himself. He was not yet thirteen.

After several months of this arrangement, the Lambs invited him to move into their home and they treated him as a son. They had no children and he did become as a son to them, establishing a relationship that would last a lifetime. Lamb would take Bob with him to the fields and woods and teach him to observe nature as an artist did.

Bob learned the langwage of painting becoming aware of colors, perspective, textures, and composition. In the cold and wet months, Lamb would teach him portrait and still life painting in his studio. People would come to the studio to pose for their portraits. There was good money in this but people were often very hard to please. They wanted to look more handsome or beautiful than they were! The successful artist was able to compromise so as to please his clients. Bob did not think this was an area of art that he would concentrate on though he wanted to learn all he could.

Lamb's home and studio, at that time, was not far from the Webb farm, and on days that Lamb had business in town, Bob went home. Indeed Mr Lamb encouraged him to do so. He was able to continue helping his mother with egg deliveries, and also the baking of bread. On weekends he continued working with his father on the construction of a tenant house, thus becoming a good carpenter and learning enough to be able, at a future time, to build a house-many houses- on his own. In advanced years he could proudly claim to have built eleven houses in his lifetime. Some were for himself and some for other people, "just because they needed them!" he proclaimed.

Chapter 6

Robert Webb, Jr. was probably fourteen years old when John Singer Sargent returned to America to complete his work on the Boston Public Library mural he had been commissioned to do. Sargent put the word out that he was looking for a young apprentice who could mix colors, keep track of his materials, and help him with installing his paintings in the library. Fred Lamb and Sargent had gone to school together in Paris and were friends. Lamb thought it was a great opportunity for Bob. It would give him a wider scope of experience in mural painting with a man of international reputation. So, he gave his best apprentice to Sargent, and Bob was off again on the train to Boston. This time he would be staying there and literally living in the Boston

Public Library.

John Singer Sargent was also one of the finest portrait painters of the day. The husbands of society women paid handsomely to have their wives' portraits painted by him. The women themselves sought him out, and gave parties for his attention and commitment to do their portraits. When he met Bob, he was trying to keep up with these demands while fulfilling his obligation to the library. When completed, the library mural would be considered by the critics of the day as one of the finest narrative paintings of this period. In addition to these assignments Sargent was commissioned to do a full length portrait of President Theodore Roosevelt. Today it hangs in the White House.

In 1912 on a cold day with broken rain clouds that hung over the bright, multi-colored fall landscape of New England, Bob Webb took an afternoon train to Boston, taking all he had in the world with him in a cloth bag. He was happy. The future looked very promising to him. He also felt good knowing he would continue to have Mr. Lamb as his mentor and friend. Lamb always said he was loaning him to someone, not giving him away. There would be many occasions when the two would come back together for work and friendship.

It would have been difficult to guess that Sargent was sixty years old. He had boundless energy and dedication to his work. When they first met at the library, Sargent asked Bob where he would be staying that night. Bob told him he had nowhere to stay and no money to rent a room. Bob already knew that Sargent didn't intend to pay him anything; no one would ever pay an apprentice to learn, even if they worked hard, and did work in addition, for their master. But he was a bit surprised when Sargent waved his hand to the stairs and said, "There, you can sleep under the stairs and use the painting ground cloths to cover the floor."

Without further ado, Sargent left for one of his nightly parties. He was a reluctant party-goer; however, the party givers added fuel to the portrait profits he was making. His clientel constantly vied for his attention. His mother and sister, who traveled with him, frequently accompanied him, though his mother, who had been born in America, preferred the social life of the continent over that of New York or Boston.

Sargent had been assigned a large room in the library to decorate. The theme of the painting was 'The Origin of Religion in the Western World'. He had traveled to Egypt and the Holy Land to get resource material and translate it into sketches. For twenty five years he traveled between London and the United States to work on the Boston library project. Though he'd enjoyed all aspects of it, he was now anxious to get it finished.

On a good working day Bob and Sargent could work nonstop until there was no more natural light. John Sargent had done the whole painting of the mural in England and brought it over in pieces to be assembled and glued to the ceiling, walls, and alcoves of the library. It was Bob's job to mix the colors to match perfectly these seam areas where the pieces came together. Sargent had the job of matching brush strokes and textures crossing the original squares now in place, so as to hide where they met. He stood on a ladder with Bob just beneath him handing him pots of paint as he asked for them.

Sargent took care of his own brushes by sticking them into the band of the hat he always wore while working. Bob thought he looked like an Indian in a war bonnet when the band was full. He also wore a vest that he cleaned his brushes on; rather than to use cleaning cloths! After a time, the vest grew saturated and colorful with pigments. Yet he would leave the library and go out to a party almost every night. Whether he went somewhere to change clothes first, Bob never knew. He often came back to the library looking the same and still wearing the same painted vest. He was a 'dry smoker' and kept the same cigar in his mouth, more or less chewing on it, all day long. He also had a red beard and an unrully crop of red hair that stuck out from beneath his bowler hat with its band of brushes. He never talked to Bob while working and rarely had anything to say to him.

After Sargent left, his young apprentice was starved. He had not been employed for money for some time and couldn't go out and buy himself a meal. He went to restaurants and asked if he could do the dishes or bus tables for something to eat. If one place turned him down, he went to another. He kept this up night after night until he could get a weekend off to go home to see if his father or Mr. Lamb might have some work for him to do, for pay. He would work for the two days only, as he intended to return to Boston and Mr. Sargent. He was already learning a lot and eating wasn't the most important thing to him.

The first weekend Mr. Sargent told him he could take a couple of days off, he headed for home. Packing up his dirty clothes, which he knew his mother would wash for him, he used the return train ticket he'd bought when he first came to his new job in Boston, and headed for Methuen. He had only a few changes of clothing plus the basics of toilet articles. He was excited to tell his family about his new apprentice work and to tell them about his boss who was a very famous artist. He also hoped to pick up work that would pay him enough so that he could buy meals without working nights to pay for them.

It was early winter, and when he arrived home it had turned bitter cold. Mystic Lake was frozen solid, and the ice cutters were signing up men to take part in this annual community project. They paid well as they should for they made a good profit from the sale of blocks of ice. The work was at once dangerous, exhilarating, fun, and a neighborhood get-together. Bob was home just in time for it. There was snow in the air as he left the house and walked a half mile to the lake. At a distance he could see the red hot barrel with fire in it that kept the men warm. All were glad to see Bob and started vying for who could get him on their team as he was well-coordinated and had almost grown into his man's height in the past year. He had slimmed down a lot from his boyhood weight yet could be counted on to carry his load.

The horses, harnessed and ready for their important part of the job, were out on the ice, whinnying, prancing and snorting steam from their nostrils, anxious to get started. Bob took his assigned position on the rear of the cutter sled, behind the driver and above the long cutting blades. Once on the sled, his job was to lean out, well over the frozen lake, which was deep right up to the edge of the bank, and thrust the forceps they handed him into the blocks of ice being cut.

As Bob told the story, the driver cracked his whip and the horses stampeded just as a great cracking sound was heard. All hearts stopped. The ice parted and a wide black hole commenced to swallow screaming horses and men, the sled, and a tangle of reins, saws and other paraphernalia. Bob and the driver shot straight upward off their seats. Bob was behind the driver and in a split second decision he reached out and pushed the driver forward with all his strength. Already high in the air, the driver went over the front grab-bar of the sled and landed sideways across the backs of the horses. It was just as Bob wanted, with little time to think. He knew the driver couldn't swim and would now be guaranteed an early rescue along with the horses.

Bob himself, however, didn't have enough forward thrust to follow the driver over the railing and splashed down sideways just over the sinking sled. Horses were always rescued first, as a team of horses cost eight hundred dollars, whereas a hired man cost just fifty cents an hour. Presumably, men could take care of themselves. The driver needed to fall with the horses to keep from drowning or being cut badly by the huge blades, had he fallen straight down.

Prepared for such disasters, the men on shore had ropes, planks, and everything they needed to lasso horses and pull them in. As they beached the thrashing animals, they were grateful to see the driver bob out of the water as well. He was twisted about with harness and hanging onto a horse's mane for dear life. They patted him down, wrapped him in a blanket, gave him a shot of rum, and sent him home.

Having jettisoned to the side, Bob had enough momentum to plunge into the great black hole. With a couple of strong kicks, he was free of the sinking sled. He could swim, but it did no good. He tried climbing onto the frozen ice separating him from the shore. Each time, his weight broke it off. The distance was too great and the water too cold. It seemed to be taking forever for the rescuers to reach him. He finally lost all strength and could no longer tread water. He breathed in water and sank below the surface unconscious. They finally retrieved him and laid him up on the bank, covering him over with a black, greasy tarp. Thinking him dead, they pulled it up over his head.

Someone went to fetch his mother. She came roaring down the hill shouting, "My poor Rob! What have they done to my baby?" Pulling back the tarp, she thought he was dead. She cried out, fainted, and dropped her considerable weight on his chest. He began to sputter and cough; water spurted from his mouth. His mother rose up and began a tirade of profanities that she could only have learned from the sailors on board their ship from England ! She was furious with the ice-master for allowing her son to nearly drown. All were afraid of her and pulled away leaving her to attend her son. She gathered him up and got him to walk home where she fed him chicken broth, warmed him and put him to bed. He would be alright in the morning.

Chapter 7

It was Saturday and Bob had another day before his return to Boston. Race day was a special day for his mother, made doubly important by the saving of her son. She was a known horse woman. Although heavy looking, she was quite short and qualified to be a jockey. She was an excellent rider. No one could outmaneuver Hannah Webb in riding, or in buying or training a horse. She knew her horseflesh; she knew a champion racehorse when she saw one, and would employ all manner of ethical, and not so ethical, means of acquiring an animal she wanted. She then would spend considerable time trying to convince the community she had been rooked in the deal; cheated worse than she ever had been before. "This horse was half blind and couldn't see to find his feed trough," she would say. When it came time to enter her horse in one of the many races held in the county, after much good training, she would persuade her family to bet heavily on it. What she went through to increase her odds nearly always proved worthwhile.

Everyone gathered down on the road where the race was to begin. The barbershop, across the street, was the bookies' station. Bets were placed until the last minute and the Webb horse was not favored to win. All shouted and jumped up and down as the horses rounded the half mile turn field and headed back home. Ma Webb with whip in hand, nudged her horse from the middle of the pack until he overtook the front runner and pulled ahead by a neck. She won and said she owed it to her anger that there were men who would allow her son to die in order to first save a team of horses. Most were sympathetic with her, thinking it could have been one of their own with less good luck.

Bob used a small portion of his pay from the ice team master to place a bet on his mother's horse to win at ten to one odds, due to her having run down her horse. She'd circulated a rumor that he could not see well and needed to follow another horse to find his way! Bob was happy to be able to take a little more money back to Boston with him. He was happy to have collected any pay at all for this near-death experience; the team master had gladly paid him rather than have an argument with Mrs. Webb.

In addition to this windfall of money he had also found another means of earning a little extra. He had met a man by the name of Ned Nixon who painted flag poles. He showed Bob how to climb a pole with just a single rope while carrying a bucket of white paint. Bob had gone around Boston a few times on Saturdays, painting poles Ned had arranged for him to do. He didn't like the work. It was dangerous and especially so if the weather turned bad. Now that he had extra change he would thank Ned but not climb any more poles. One near miss with his life was enough.

Bob enjoyed his mother's victory celebration. Now that he was old enough, his father poured him a glass of rum in the local pub where they stopped on their way home from the races. That night, Bob was happy to eat a snack his sister Jane had prepared for him. They were all looking at him as a hero, having heard the story from the sled driver who had been saved by Bob's quick action. Even his older brothers stopped by and gave him slaps and condolences for what he had gone through. They had a new respect for their younger brother. Though he did nothing to save his own life, he had been spared. Everyone was amazed at the carelessness of those checking the temperature and condition of the lake. The company would be suspect from now on. Only good fortune or providence had kept anyone from losing his life. Bob would remember this company and its lost reputation for a lifetime.

Though the Webbs were not a deeply religious family, this brush with death woke a pensive regard for the unknown. Their mother acted for all of them and went to the Christian Science Church to give thanks for her son's life. Bob gave some thought to it, but for now he had a job to do and he couldn't dwell on it. The young art apprentice took the night train back to Boston. He knew his time with a truly great master, John Singer Sargent, was short, and he intended to get all he could out of it.

The job was nearly done; he knew that Sargent wanted to go to war. England had already entered the war raging in Europe. He unrolled the ground cloth he used to sleep on under the stairs. It had become more comfortable due to the generous gift of an extra blanket and a feather pillow from the night watchman. The old gentleman had been very kind to him bringing him sandwiches, on occasion, when he knew Bob was hungry.

Events of the past few days occupied Bob's mind and prevented sleep. He wondered about his future and what plans he might make to advance his career as an artist. His apprenticeship with Sargent was coming to an end and he would very soon be looking for a new assignment. Few people could make a full time living as an artist and he recalled that Mr. Lamb also worked as a teacher, Melby was a house painter-- among other things of which Bob knew very little. Sargent was...and he heard the front door of the library open quietly and someone assended the stairs. Sargent was "home" from one of his parties. He frequently came back to the library to have a final look at his work before going to his rooming house for the night. He turned on the lights and walked around examining his efforts of the day before.

Another click of the door was heard and someone ascended the stairs; this time it was the night watchman. Bob rolled over and out of his cocoon and up on his feet letting it be known he was the third of this midnight gathering. The two gentlemen laughed when they saw him and he figured he must be a sight in his longjohns and his hair standing on end. Sargent asked the watchman if he had heard the news? "America is at war!" Sargent said gleefully. He wanted America to be in the war. The three men exchanged views on the event, speculating as to what it would mean for each of them. They then split up and went their separate ways.

Bob rolled back under the stairs and in a flash of enlightenment he knew he had his answer as to what he would be doing in the forseeable future. He would go into the military service. Like his immigrant parents, he had a strong love for the nation and would do anything to defend her and preserve what she stood for. Meanwhile he had a job to complete and a night's sleep to put in.

John Singer Sargent continued to stay out quite late at night going to various parties to which he was invited. His clientele of prominent people gradually became bothersome to him. He invented a name for these fashionable American tycoons he had come to resent. They were "mugs" he would be painting to help assure their place in society with their use of his name.

He could not deny their importance to him, however. His mother often reminded him of his responsibility for having been given so great a talent. Such sentiment was hers, not his, and he knew that the library commission meant most to him and that time spent on it was, in part, made possible by his portrait work. He could not possibly ask the full amount in pay for the hours and hours spent on the library. He could, and did ask a very high price for the portraits of the beautiful ladies of Boston and New York.

After better than a year, Sargent was pleased that his young apprentice had developed such skill in matching colors. He also believed that the young man could paint and decided to give him a chance to do so. When , after a day on the ladder and reaching up, Sargent felt very tired, he thought now was the time. He took off his hat and pulled the brushes from the band they were stuck in and handed them over to Bob. At first astonished, Bob knew this could mean only one thing and he simply took them, climbed the ladder, and went to work! An act of tremendous faith on Sargent's part, this did wonders to boost Bob's confidence. He felt that he had come into his own and could take on any assignment given him from now on.

One day while working on the ladder Sargent looked down at his apprentice standing on the floor with pots of paint around him and said, " I have something to say to you young man." This was rare for Sargent as he never talked while working. "Yes Sir?" Bob replied, "Young man, would you like to go back to England with me?" he asked. "Then, after the war you could continue your apprenticeship. We'd first go off to the war together and have a bully of a good time." It sounded exciting and Bob told Mr. Sargent so but, to himself, he had reservations. He felt that if he was going to fight in a war, he would want to fight for his own country.

Trench fighting may not have turned out so well for the young American. He stayed alive and had his own vision of painting to look forward to. In the future, when he had time to do easel painting, his works were colorful with some of the airial freedom of brushstroke as seen in transitional works of the 20th Century, as well as in the works of Sargent. The idea of resuming his apprenticeship after the war was appealing and he would talk it over with his folks.

That weekend when Bob went home, he told his mother what Sargent had said. His mother's response could be heard all the way to the cattle barn. "No son of mine will ever fight in a European war!" she shouted, "We left England to get away from all their troubles." That was that, and Bob didn't want to go with Sargent anyway. His mother never interfered with his work but he was not altogether surprised to see her one day soon after that in the library in Boston. He steered her away from Sargent, fearing she would give him a piece of her mind for trying to persuade her son to go off to a war in Europe.

She had been so animated with anger Bob didn't know what she might do. He quickly gave her a grand tour of the library, pointing out what he had done to help with the painting on walls and ceiling. She was so thrilled by seeing his work, and that of Sargent, that she forgot her original mission-if she had one- and expressed her pride in her son.

On another occasion, his sister Jane, who was working as a private nurse in Boston, came by to visit him and waited until lunchtime so that she might take him out to eat. He had other visitors who meant much to him. Bob was a people person and needed people around him. His old friends from Methuen dropped in to check out this famous ceiling painting they had read about in the newspapers. Everyone used discretion, not wanting to interfere with the work going on. They would not have been allowed to anyway, with cordoned off work areas keeping library patrons at a distance.

They stood by, out of range, until he had been given permission to leave for lunch or at the end of the day. These times of being with his friends meant much to him. He also looked forward to the change of pace and chance to see the city of Boston. They frequently took a trolley and toured the waterfront and various places of interest.

His apprenticeship was going fast and as it was coming to the end he knew he had gained confidence and new skills he could take with him. He now had tools of his trade that he would use for a lifetime. In fact he had gone beyond a mere Apprentice and accomplished what then was known as a level of Journeyman. To be a Master was the last rung on this ladder of achievment. He aspired to reach such a high and lofty goal and felt confident that, with experience and maturity-and perhaps a break here and there- he would someday succeed.

The next day, back at the library, they had a surprise visit by a master painter, Mr. Lamb. Bob continued to address him respectfully as ' Mr. Lamb' for a lifetime. He was surprised somehow to see his old mentor. He had not seen Lamb for a long time. They greeted each other warmly and Lamb assured him he would be back to spend time with him after first visiting with his old friend John Sargent. He and Sargent left the library together with Sargent telling Lamb he had something he wanted to talk over with him.

When they returning Sargent looked at the clock and gave Bob leave to go to lunch with his old friend. Lamb took him to a casual resturant near the Museum of Fine Arts and afterward dropped him off at the library again. Upon leaving, he said that he would expect to see him soon back home in Methuen. In a day or two after that they completed the work at the library and Bob's final duty was to help with the cleaning up. He helped Sargent pack materials to be shipped back to England and as a final gesture of 'thank you', and good will, Sargent gave Bob a small pastel drawing he had done.

Bob kept the pastel for his lifetime, until it became so faded and blended in color that the subject matter could no longer be distinguished. It faintly appeared to have been three dancing figures. He wondered why he had never taken care of it and had it framed ! It meant something to him and he always kept it in a chest along with important papers. Bob tried to restore it with little success. It had moved , too many times, with him. He finally gave it away to an old friend, who asked him for it. Sargent had not signed it as he had rarely signed any of his work. On the back he wrote,"To my friend Bobby."

Sargent bid goodbye to his young apprentice, attended a farewell dinner with top government officials, visited some old friends, and with his mother and sister, sailed for London. The last thing he said to Bob was that he wanted to get into the trenches and illustrate what war was really like. This is what he did, spending some months at the front with pen and brushes, as well as rifle, in hand. The British military had overlooked his age, gave him a uniform and rifle and no doubt classified him as a war correspondent. He had been a celebrity and the pride of England for his artistic accomplishments. The military could not refuse his request.

With America mobilizing for war, like most young men, Bob wanted to go into the service. Months before his sixteenth birthday, he was unemployed, and eager for adventure and action. The excitement, glamour, and chance to see some of the world pulled the young men to the army or navy. Bob walked by the Marine Corps Recruiting Office and turned into it. He lied about his age, but it didn't matter; they didn't want him anyway. He was tall, about five ten or eleven, but as skinny as a rail. The officer told him to go home and come back when he could put on twenty pounds or more.

Chapter 8

Bob took the train to Methuen and went straight to Lamb's studio, hoping his mentor and friend might have a painting commission for him; a pub needing painting, or a public building to be decorated. He told Lamb of his experience at the recruiting office. Lamb listened attentively and could see Bob's disappointment. It was apparent he really wanted to be in the military. Lamb had wanted to hear what the young man had in mind for his future and whether he was truly interested in the military. He didn't want Bob to make a lifetime commitment to the service, but he did have something very special in mind that would require a dedication and maturity Bob may not be ready for; afterall he was just fifteen years old and would not be sixteen for several more months. He told him to sit down; he had something to tell him.

Lamb was aware of the independant spirit of his young friend. If he made a commitment to someone, or something, he would remain loyal. If however, he felt he was being used badly he would break off and go his own way. He could not have such an attitude in the service. Lamb talked to him and explained where the military was coming from with their discpline and why orders had to be followed, even if they were not agreed with or always understood. Bob was not a 'hot head' or a maverick and his own personal trials had given him the grit and stick-to-it-ness Lamb was proud of him for. Bob had matured since going to work with Sargent and he could now see him doing well in the military.

He was especially pleased that Bob had continued his dedication to the field of art. It confirmed Lamb's belief that the young man had a genuine calling. He understood this in himself. It seemed providential to him that Bob's going into the Navy, at this time, would have the gift of another new art experience that he would be explaining to him, as his friend John Sargent had explained it to him. He had no doubt that Bob would grab hold of this unique opportunity arranged by Sargent through contacts he had made with the brass in the Navy. The young man's age didn't seem relevant. It was never brought up in consideration of the position.

John Sargent, before he left, told Lamb of an encounter he had with the U.S. Secretary of the Navy who shared some interesting information with him. It seems that a new service was being set up within the Navy that would use art to protect troops, cargo and battleships from enemy torpedoes. It would be called a 'camouflage department.' The secretary asked Sargent's opinion as to what qualifications the men should have who would staff the new department. Lamb made a lengthy story of it and held out till the last telling Bob what was in store for him. Bob gave him rapt attention and began to ask questions about what 'camouflage' was and how the navy could use it to protect their ships. Lamb told him it would be up to the artist to decide how ships would be painted to fool the enemy.

Lamb could see the idea taking hold in the young man's head. Bob could hardly contain himself, he was so excited. Lamb raised a hand to quiet him down, saying, "You haven't heard all of it yet." Sargent, in answering the Secretary of the Navy's request for qualifications of men to fill this roll as camouflage artists, proposed that his young friend Robert James Webb, Jr. be put in charge of the new department! He told the secretary that Bob could set the standard for all the other recruits to the new camouflage department. Sargent offered to write Bob Webb a recommendation, which he did, there at the dinner table.

The Secretary took the recommendation and said he would forward it to the Admiral of the Fifth Naval District at Newport News, Virginia, along with a letter of his own. Lamb said he had been contacted as a second reference for Bob and had added his own name to the other two in support of his young prote'ge'. Bob's mouth dropped open; he could hardly believe what he was hearing. He then shouted with joy and jumped in the air ! What should he do? That was obvious. He would have to go to Newport News, Virginia and enlist in the navy! He knew his family would be pleased. He knew his parents would be proud of him.

They were all jubilant; Bob because he would be doing what he was trained to do; his mother because he wouldn't be going into combat; his father was proud that he would be serving his country and also have a regular paying job; and his sister and brothers felt that he deserved the break he was getting because he'd been through many challenges in his young life, but had kept on going and had his sense of humor. They all knew he had worked hard and deserved this break that now came his way.

His sister Jane teased him about how handsome he would look in his new uniform. She predicted that he would have many girlfriends, but he only blushed at this. A handsome youth, he had dark neatly combed hair, light blue eyes, a wide expressive mouth and classic straight nose. Girls were only a secondary part of his life. He certainly noticed them as they did him, but he didn't have the time and didn't want to be distracted by them. The girls he knew were the sisters of his buddies. Everyone did things together as a group, going to the flicks, ice skating, horse races, county fairs, and the like.

He liked women who, on their own, accomplished something. The women in his family were strong individuals, and he admired them. His aunt Ett was a suffragette and went to many rallies and marches. She was one of the first women in the country to drive a motor car; her husband was glad to loan her his machine as she was also a good mechanic. As many women who could drive in the 1920's, she had learned how to repair the motor if anything went wrong. Women felt a great independance by driving whereever they pleased and the suffregetts often drove their husbands cars to their meetings.

Aunt Ett was also a prohibitionist and her efforts as such often disturbed many a bar owner. She carried bricks in a basket and thought nothing of shattering a large plateglass window. Bob's mother and sister were also free spirits doing pretty much as they pleased. He knew his mother was the one who ran things in their family, though his father had the last word if a question was to be settled. His sister was ambitious as well. In later years she would open the first nursing home for the elderly in Florida.

In character, Robert Webb Jr. was his mother's son, with firm convictions and a stubborn tenacity. His father taught him self control and a strong work ethic. Mr. Lamb had been like a wise uncle to him, as well as teacher. The Navy would challenge him, and he knew it would change him, having seen a difference in his friends when they came home on leave. He trusted that the Navy would use his talent and even help him develop it. He couldn't wait to leave.

Bob should have gotten written permission from his father to join the navy, as he was under the required age. Robert James Senior could neither read nor write, and they simply forgot it. Robert James Jr. had no trouble advancing his age by a year on the recruiting forms. He was going to have a position that required more maturity, and he reasoned that he would be a year older very soon anyway. What difference did it make whether he waited a few months or enlisted when he knew he was ready?

His family gathered around him at the train station and they all hugged him, shook his hand and his mother kissed him "goodbye" as the train puffed into the station. Even his father came to see him off to basic training. The nation was at war, and the future was uncertain. No one could guess what was in store for young Robert Webb. He was probably as well prepared, or better, than most to enter this demanding life of a sailor. He eagerly looked forward to the experience.

Chapter 9

The ride through the countryside was slow, with many stops. They called this a "milk train" because it stopped at every cow pasture along the way; or possibly, it did pick up metal containers of milk and drop them off at the next town. The cool, lush green of the north finally gave way to the languid, humid, density of the south. The train had chugged through the hills and valleys of New York and on south till reaching Maryland. Here they skirted around some waterways and Bob thought Maryland was a very beautiful state.

Next they crossed a wide river, probably the Potomac, and were in Virginia. For Bob, it was love at first sight when he saw Virginia. It had a feeling of being the south and he appreciated the warmth, after bone chilling, sub-zero temperatures of Massachusettes. The vegetation had struggled through high heat and won a right to its year round foliage. Homesteads were neat and clean; people and animals in the fields moved slowly. Some of the boys who got on the train even talked slower!

The train suddenly came to a screeching stop with the sound of metal sliding against metal. Their military officer came through and told everybody to get off the train. They would have two hours in this little town while a flat tire on the train got fixed! The whistle would blow once when they had five minutes left to get back. Two whistles, and the train was leaving. The flat tire meant that an overheated wheel had actually melted down and gone flat! That was a new one to Bob, who had been riding trains since a boy.

As Bob walked through the small village of Williamsburg, Virginia, he had no idea he was walking through the place where he would spend the last thirty plus years of his life. This was long before John D. Rockefeller had bought up most of the old houses and remade the city to look as it did back in the 1770's. It had been the capital of the nation then, and the home of Thomas Jefferson and Patrick Henry. George Washington had walked its streets. American independence was conceived here in the Raleigh Tavern where these great men met to discuss the course of the then thirteen colonies toward unity.

Most of the recruits did not know the history of the town. The one or two local boys who did know would educate others. What he saw were sheep grazing on a village green, old houses, and very ancient looking buildings. It had a charm and relaxed atmosphere about it. Just ordinary working people were going about their business. It didn't take long to walk from one end of the Duke of Glouster Street, as the main street in town was called, to the other, before they heard the train whistle sound once. The boys all took off running. No one wanted to miss his induction into the Navy.

Bob had no trouble passing the physical and other tests. He wondered why they spent time inquiring as to his other interests and abilities. He told them he liked to cook and bake; he was especially proud of this, knowing not many young men could cook. He told them of helping his father build a house. He was good with animals and could garden and do any number of other things a boy learns on the farm. He didn't tell them about his skill as an artist because he thought they already knew this! He thought he would go directly into the Camouflage Department. When they assigned him to the commissary to do the cooking, he was more than surprised !

The Navy had not made it comfortable for

them. Their immediate barracks were in an abandoned peanut warehouse. They slept on the floor with bags of peanuts piled high all around. Of course they ate too many of them and got sick. Such peanuts as these were never known at home, unroasted and right out of the fields. Maybe something was just going around that caused them all to get sick. The barracks were getting awfully crowded and the heat of the south and the stench of sickness made it almost unbearable. More recruits were signing up than the military had facilities for. However, the peanut warehouse didn't last long. Waterfront housing and naval offices were soon made available on the Chesapeake Bay front. In the future, the Camouflage Art Department would also have their studios here, as well as the photography department.

Bob was a good cook, praised by enlisted men and officers alike. He really didn't mind the mix up in assignment as he was hungry from the years of apprenticing without any pay. However, several weeks went by with his preparing huge quantities of food and receiving promises that his new camouflage assignment was coming. He received no training by the Navy to be a cook. He did what came naturally, as he had learned in his mother's kitchen. When he didn't have something he found out how to get it. He made up his own menus, recalling what big hungry farm hands liked to eat. Those working with him soon fell in line, following him in planning and preparing meals. When he left for his camouflage assignment he felt he would be leaving a trained crew behind.

Officers began asking for special foods. The Captain ordered a steak and was pleased to have it prepared to perfection. He wanted to know who was in the kitchen saying to be sure to keep him. Mealtime was looked forward to by everyone-officers and enlisted men alike. They even got hot fresh baked bread daily ! Bob was eating better and putting on a bit of weight, which he could use. He woke up to the fact, however, that he was not doing what he signed up to do and he wondered if the recommendations Mr. Lamb told him about had really been sent? He finally decided to take some action. The meals would become less palatable. After a time, they would be downright repulsive. He would no longer bake bread every day. He would allow the meals to sit and get cold before serving them. He knew he would no longer be popular, but that would be all right if he could get his transfer.

When he got paid he got a pass to go out into the city of Newport News and find an art supply store. He bought a sketch book, pencils, pens and ink and some drafting tools. In his spare time he began to draw. He also began to ask questions. His officer over him picked up his cause.

At the same time matters of security were developing on the Chesapeake. Robert Webb got his transfer. Commander Bushnell was over Naval Intelligence as well as the new Camouflage Department. He could use the young self-assured and talented seaman Webb in both capacities. A very serious problem had come up where the German submarines were entering the Chesapeake Bay and running up the James River. Intelligence knew they were surfacing and landing men. It was assumed that these men infiltrated into the community and probably met with local German sympathizers. Intelligence needed to know what they were up to, other than a good German home cooked meal.

A large German community existed in the Tidewater area, having been there since the Revolutionary War era when the Hessian soldiers fought against the revolutionaries as mercenaries supporting the British. Bushnell decided to send seaman Webb into the community, appearing as a native who belonged there. Bob was to get friendly with the locals and gain their confidence. Hopefully, someone would tell him something about the German movements.

Young Webb traded his Navy uniform for

civilian clothes and went out looking for work. He learned that there was to be a dance locally that he would be able to attend. Returning to his ship he reported this to Officer Bushnell, who gave him instructions on what to do. He went to the dance and was grateful to his sister Jane for having taught him how to dance. This was not a bad job! He thought it was much better than working over hot stoves. The Chesapeake weather was hot and muggy enough, especially in this James River valley full of swamps.

What he looked forward to was meeting some pretty girls and getting to dance with them. This he did. Further, he learned from them that a young stranger at the dance confided that he had sailed a long way on a ship just to visit the girls. They giggled and thought this was just a line to appear important to them. Bob knew better. He knew he was onto something when they added that the stranger had a funny accent. He decided he would discretely follow the young bragging German, after the dance.

He was led to a remote inlet in the James River where he watched several young men from the dance get into a small craft and push out to the middle of the river. It was dark but with just enough moonlight to see. They began to row and made little effort to be quiet. This was an isolated area of the tidewater with no residences up close to the shore. Bob had no trouble following at a safe distance so as not to be seen. The boys were too occupied with recounting their exploits at the dance.

Tailing them was not easy as there was no real footpath on the bank. Brush was high and thick and he had to keep oriented by where the water's edge was. The ground here was saturated to a point were Bob continually got stuck in the mud. Mosquitoes buzzed around his head, and now and then a night bird would screech and take off ahead of him. He feared the young boat passengers would wonder what had alarmed the birds. He knew they were a bit drunk and hoped this would save him from detection.

Finally they stopped rowing, in the middle of the river, and stood up. They dismounted from their skiff and seemed to be standing up on the water! They then disappeared. It was very dark now that the moon had gone down, but Bob figured they were standing on a submarine and then had descended down inside of it. He waited a minute and saw the small boat they had come in drift away. He searched his way back to his base reflecting all the while that this was not an easy assignment after all.

So much of the land along the bank was swamp

marshland. More than once he had gone into the water and had to extricate a foot or a whole leg from a sinkhole that sucked him down. It was cold with a penetrating dampness. The air was filled with diving bats as well as masquitos that he could not swat for fear of making noise. Furthermore he took a circuitous route back to the base so as not to get caught; and it took him twice as long to reach the barracks. He had been instructed what to do if he did get caught. One thing for sure was that he would not confess to being in the Navy. He had figured that out for himself.

The next day Bushnell sent him out again, this time to tail the Germans and determine who the Americans were who were with them. He was given an officers uniform and sent to another party. He felt assured by the snappy clean, white, uniform that this would not be another night of adventure along the banks of the James River. There he met other officers whom he assumed were genuine real naval officers and was given instructions by them. Like himself they had been given warrents for arrest, and weapons. After some reconnaissance, which included going to a movie theater,when the time came they were able to identify the Americans who were aiding the enemy. Bob simply said,"We rounded them up and brought them in."

Anything further of this adventure ended

abruptly here. Bob said no more and when pressed to do so pleaded that anything further was secret classified information. Some sixty years later, in telling the story he finally added, after some coaxing, that they had been successful. We didn't learn from him what, if anything, happend to the Germans. We couldn't read meaning in his far off look, and the abrupt twinkle in his eye. What transpired militarily probably did end there and was secret. By now it is possibly declassified and may be read in the naval archives. His oath of silence remained intact all these many years.

Years later, shortly after Bob's death, a large envelope arrived in the mail, at his home in Virginia, addressed to his then wife and with a return address simply saying, "The White House." Inside was a certificate with the gold presidential seal honoring the memory of Robert J. Webb for his "...devotion and selfless service to our county while in the armed forces..." It was signed by Ronald Reagan, President of the United States. Bob would have been so proud, and pleased as Ronald Reagan was his favorite president. Whatever his assignment was all those many years ago he was successful and the country remembered him.

Nothing was done about the submarines within the bay during that war to end all wars, the First World War, as our military knew that to sink them would block the waterway, and no ships could pass through it thereafter. Interestingly this same problem was encountered by our revolutionaries at the Battle of Yorktown in about 1780, as was told to Bob by Commander Bushnell, a history buff. It wasn't, of course submarines our forces feared then but rather the British navy. Bob had heard of Lafayette and what he had done to get the French fleet there in time to scatter the British fleet before they could enter the bay. Bushnell gave Bob a history lesson by telling him that, "the British could not resupply their ground troops, at Yorktown, because they were unable to get their supply ships in to dock and unload. Neither could the British retreat by the sea. That was a deciding factor in the American's winning at the battle of Yorktown and thereby winning the Revolution.

Our American military did not allow the German submarines freedom to simply slip away back to their homeland. Many ships were attacked after leaving, or before entering the Chesapeake Bay. This is where the navy balloon came into play. Bob, having gone up several times, said it was very easy to see below the water at that height. The United States established a German cemetary, in the Bay area, for those Germans having lost their lives in American waters and on our shores.

Chapter 10

The older officer was fond of this young recruit. He was forever amazed at how quickly he coud grasp an idea and with energy and willingness accept an assignment. He could trust young Webb to carry out anything given to him to do. Seaman Webb, on the other hand had great respect for his commanding officer and would have followed him 'into hell' as he stated. Bushnell was the gold standard in Bobs eyes. In 1918 when Officer Busnell and his subordinate Webb stood at a ships rail and looked out over this beautiful natural harbor, the largest seaport and shipbuilding pride of the nation, America was fully into the First World War. There was little time to train a recruit in all the details of his assignment. An intelligence officer had to pick his men and trust he had been right about their background and experience in the outside world. Thus it was that Bob was picked for another naval intellegence undercover operation.

A seaman while on shore leave had killed a civilian in a bar fight. The Navy was required to send him back to the First Naval District in Boston for incarceration and trial. Bushnell called Bob in for this assignment. He would be shackled to the prisoner and put on a train north. The train would make stops along the way, one of which, the prisoner later told Bob, was his home town. The prisoner had not been home for years to see his widowed mother who lived alone.

Bob had a gift, or an intuitive sense, beyond his years, for recognizing people for what they really were, rather than what they wanted others to believe of them. This fellow was in remorse now that he was sober. It wasn't the first time he had been in trouble, but this was the worst with the greatest consequences. He was truly not an evil young man, but what he had done in a drunken moment could cost him his life. Bob felt for him and thought of what such a thing would mean to himself and to his own mother. In this case, the boy's mother should never know the story. Bob already knew what he had in mind, but determined he could not tell the prisoner until after the fact of their standing at her doorstep.

When they came to the town claimed to be his mother's, Bob pulled the sleeping prisoner to his feet and to the exit door of the train. He knew they could get on the next train through in two hours time, having studied the train schedule he picked up. He had been given an open pass which allowed him free movement as a serviceman on a government assignment. At first, the prisoner was dazed by what was happening. Bob shook him to stay awake in order to give directions to his house. In this small crossroads town, it couldn't be too far to walk anywhere. Bob had a gun belt with a small caliber pistol issued him, and was advised he could kill the prisoner if he tried to escape.

To make this detour was not a part of his orders, of course, and he had thought of how he could explain it if anything went wrong. He had made a risky decision that could end his military career, and more. He simply had put himself in the prisoner's situation, and he felt right about doing it. He thought about his own mother. This mother would never see her only son again, and one last happy memory was a gift. It reflected Bob Webb's character at once as a strength and weakness. It certainly was not acceptable Navy procedure. He trusted they would never find out.

The captor and captive were very hungry and it was about lunch time. Bob told the prisoner to close his eyes and turn his head eastward to the sun, as he fished the handcuff key out of his sock and unshackeled them. They stood in the middle of nowhere with only a few run-down houses, isolated, with nothing more than a diner, general store, and the train station nearby. Bob wondered why a train would even stop here! "Which house is your mother's ?" he demanded. The prisoner led them to the last house on the dirt path, and Bob knocked at the door. The door opened with a squeak from old hinges, and with a gasp of delight, the mother flew into the arms of her son.

After lunch and a brief visit, the two stood once again on the platform watching their train approach. The cuffs were locked and hidden with a Navy peacoat drapped over them; to prevent attention being drawn to them. Bob would need the coat in the colder Northern climate. He was familiar with where they were going and had no trouble carrying his prisoner to the naval base in Boston.

Both young men had been quiet all the way. Only now did the prisoner open up to say thank you to Bob. He had tears in his eyes as Bob turned to him and said, "I don't know anything about it, and neither must you – ever." They parted as Bob handed over the prisoner's papers to the officer in charge. He showed his own orders and was dismissed. He headed for the train station and Methuen, glad the mission was over with and successfully accomplished.

Bob had a two-day pass, and his officer, Bushnell, had told him to visit his folks before returning to base. Drained from his experience of transporting the prisoner, Bob wanted nothing more than to sit in his mother's kitchen with a cup of tea in his hand and relax. The Webbs continued their English heritage and drank tea. Bob would never change to coffee. The senior Webbs were now alone with all their children scattered in various services or employment, and in other states. After happy greetings, and catching up on the news while his mother rushed about preparing a meal for him, his father came home, and they all sat down together.

It was helpful for Bob to tell his parents of his recent assignment of bringing a prisoner to jail. His sympathy was so much with the prisoner he couldn't get him out of his head. He admitted to his mother that he wished he'd helped him escape. His mother wondered if the prisoner had asked him for any such help? Bob said he had not. His mother reminded him of the prisoner's crime, and that he had to pay for it. She had faith in the Navy's judicial system as she did in the civil courts. She felt his remorse and drunken condition would be factors in the case. She reminded Bob that he didn't know all the circumstances. His mother felt that sometimes Bob was too impulsive. She would not tell him he was wrong in what he had done, but she was worried that he was not mature enough for such an assignment. His father, who mostly sat and listened to this exchange, looked up and quietly said, "Follow your orders, son; that's what you should always do." Bob appreciated this. Hs father rarely gave him advice; he would remember it.

Chapter 11

His ability to follow orders was sorely tested not long after he reported back to the base. Bob had an art studio in an office complex on shore overlooking the bay and ships at anchor, since he'd recently been put in charge of the Camouflage Department. Officer Bushnell had been put in charge of a ship in port. When he heard that Bob was back, he came and brought him on board his ship. A crew of sailors was already aboard. When an emergency came up that required Bushnell to briefly leave the ship, he put Bob in charge, since there was no officer of rank to be responsible while he was gone.

Officer Bushnell told the crew that Seaman Robert Webb would be in command, and they were to do whatever he told them. He instructed

Bob he was not to allow anyone, no matter who they said they were, to board the ship. Shortly after Bushnell left, and Bob was now in charge, it happened that a small Navy vessel pulled up to the side and sailors climbed a ladder to board. Bob ordered his men to stand at attention and be ready to shoot anyone coming over the side! The men had been issued firearms, but had very little training in how to use them. Bob, of course, had shot a gun since he was big enough to hold one. Hunting had been a constant in his boyhood; he had always supplied the family with small game. He didn't want the game on this ship to be any of his fellow sailors, however! He trusted that nobody would be trigger happy.

It was the Admiral of the entire fleet attempting to board! His sailors tried to relay this to Bob, but he shouted that he had his orders and was serious about shooting any offender. The Admiral had to retreat and only when Officer Bushnell came back could he board his own ship! He commended Bob for sticking to his orders and would reward him later for doing so.

Bob had made a request for an additional helper in his department and, after some time went by, he was given a young seaman to work with whose father was a United States Senator. The Senator had a yacht of fairly good size and negotiated a deal whereby if his son were assigned to shore duty, or at least could be assured of a noncombatant role, he would give his ship to the Navy. Bob and the young sailor worked together on the yacht. It was made into an art studio with a photographic department.

Rear Admiral Sims gave special recognition to Bob and gave orders that the camouflage department would have top priority in getting everything they needed. Bob finally was given a pass whereby he could board any ship at any time to carry out his mission. This was something he badly needed, having spent so much time trying to find the right authority to allow him to board ships he was to survey for painting. He enjoyed the new status and special recognition he was receiving .

It was about this time that a lighter note entered their routine. Lieutenant Bushnell was to be married. He married the niece of Dr. Goodwin, pastor of the Bruton Parish Church in Williamsburg, Virginia. Bob and his new right hand helper were invited to the wedding. Bob noted that Bushnell had just then become what he called a "Three Stripper" next to Captain.

Bob fretted that he was unable to buy the couple a decent wedding gift for lack of funds. His pay was $37 a month of which $25 was taken out for insurance. In case of his death, he said, his mother would receive the money. That left him $12. What he gave them did not please him but anyone would think the young couple might be very pleased indeed. Using paints and a board found in his ships studio, he painted a seascape for them. He constructed a simple frame and the two sailors hitched a ride to the church for the wedding with Bob's painting in hand and an elegant gift from his more affluent seaman partner whose father was a U.S.Senator.

They settled into a routine of work and a great deal of protective camouflage on the United States fleet was accomplished. Ships appeared to be sailing backward. There were reconnaissance ships on the sides of battleships and illusions of ocean waves, sky and clouds, where there were none. Bob painted them realistically, and they became an illusion. The fleet took on strange appearances designed to fool the German submarine periscopes. Bob would paint the bow of a ship on the side of a larger one so as to appear to be moving straight forward toward the enemy!

These illusions had to be worked out in the studio first, in miniature, on composition panels. They were photographed and arranged and rearranged, painted and repainted many times.

New paints were experimented with to combat the erosion of salt water and salt air on metal. It was a challenging assignment in which a team of young Navy men who were artists, chemists, photographers and laborers worked together. Bob always said that he could not be credited for accomplishing anything he did, alone. Whatever he did throughout his life had always been a team effort. The efforts of this team ultimately saved many lives of those on troop carriers, battleships and wherever the Navy encountered enemy torpedo and surface fire power.

Bob carried his designs to the on land photography department where photos were taken and a record file kept. Copies were made to help the artists save time in experimenting with cut and paste, trial and error, color and shape manipulations. It was during one of these trips that Bob met a young lady who would change his life. Her name was Rosa, and she was an employee in the photography department. He walked by her desk and a soft scent of lavender caught his attention. She was very pretty. He turned around and retraced his steps to pass by her again. This time she looked up at him and smiled. He saw that she was not just pretty but beautiful! Something happened to him, and he knew that he would need a lot more work from the photography department.

When he reached out and handed her his negatives, he said, "I need these to be developed today." She asked him to be seated and left the room with them. He hoped that she would come right back. He wanted to talk with her while the developer worked magic on the film. He never thought he had any magic with women, but something worked in his favor that day. She did come back, and they struck up a conversation that would go on for fifty years!

They both had big responsibilities in their respective naval assignments but managed to take their times off together. Summers in tidewater Virginia were best enjoyed in early evening and they took walks, boat rides, and found quiet places where they could be together. Magnolia trees were still in bloom and their sweet smell permeated the air. Dogwood trees had lost their blossoms trading them for a rich, bright green follage. A breeze off the water was refreshing. They had become totally consumed--with each other. They were in love.

Rosa was from North Carolina and in the coming year, on several occasions, Bob had gone there with her to meet her family. There was no question of their future together. When

Bob's two year tour of duty, plus one year in the reserves , was nearly up, he asked Rosa to marry him.   His discharge papers said, "Honorably Discharged Due to Insufficient Funds."   The government had run out of money to support its armed forces. They had won the war, but the nation was left in a great depression.

The couple first went to North Carolina where they were married. From there they headed to Boston where Bob felt sure he could get employment as a painter; painting houses if nothing else came along. He had no civilian clothes and no money to buy any. Like many veterans, he would wear his uniform until it wore out. He had no job and no prospects for one and neither did his wife, who was already pregnant.

Chapter 12

People in the Boston area were hungry, as everywhere else in the nation. There was no work, the mills had closed as war contracts had ceased. Bob would have to make his own job if he couldn't find one. Things were so desperate people had begun to steal from the farmers. Chickens, livestock, anything in the ground was confiscated in the nighttime. Bob's uncle had a prosperous farm and he asked Bob to be a night watchman for him. Each night he would walk around the farm and outbuildings, the chicken coop, the barn, and the gardens. The walk was long and cold as winter came on, and the pay was short and insufficient to meet his needs. Something would have to be done.

Rosa was pregnant and needed to eat enough for the baby. When the time came they were not worried about the delivery, Bob's mother was a midwife and would be delivering the baby as she had taken care of many of the women in this rural community. They had to eat and, out of desperation, Bob came to a decision. That night, a heavy snow blanketed the ground as he made his usual rounds with the last check being at the chicken coop. It was very dark, very late and blustery. The wind cut his face, and he was grateful for his Navy peacoat, the warmest coat he had ever had. His legs and feet were frozen, however.

Taking the padlock on the chicken coop in hand, as if to examine it, he swiftly inserted a metal point and gave a turn. It popped open and he released it from the door frame and entered. The birds were asleep and not too bothered by this intrusion. He quickly lifted a fat one from her perch, slipped a rubber band around the beak, secured her legs and tucked her inside his peacoat. He had a gunny sack secured at his waist, much as he always did when hunting for rabbits, and dropped the hen inside. His footprints had to look normal requiring that he continue his nightly rounds and exit by the road, as usual.

Bob's uncle, at his upstairs bedroom window,

checked each morning for his nephew's footprints of the night before. He did not go out to check the outbuildings however, thus never missed the hen or several more through that cold Massachusetts winter. He felt that with his nephew as night watchman, his property was secure from the marauding scavengers from the city.

When he wanted a chicken for dinner he asked Bob to catch one and prepare it for him. The stock went down in numbers and Bob reported such to his uncle attributing the depletion to foxes that frequented the woods around the farm. Foxes indeed! Bob had learned a few of that little animal's ways.

Bob's parents had a cottage they were unable to rent, noone could pay any rent, and they gave it to Bob and Rosa. Robert Senior felt they could arrange to pay as they were able from the small wage received from Uncle David. It had a basement with a dirt floor. Whenever Bob gave himself a bonus of a chicken, he took a shovel to the basement and plucked and gutted and buried all evidence of it. By the end of winter, the basement had many little mounds carefully smoothed over and hardly visible.

Uncle David occasionally came calling; Bob and Rosa wanted no visible signs of the many chicken dinners they had from the farm. After dinner even the bones from the carcasses were buried. Mother Webb knew what was going on and was happy to cooperate, saying that the old miser should be paying Bob more money anyway. They were all trying to help each other through those hard times, except for Uncle David. The family story was that when he finally died, he had made his own casket and it was so heavy ten men could hardly lift it off the floor. They jokingly concluded he had made a false bottom in it and filled it with his gold.

After that long hard winter on the farm during which Bob had continually made contacts with his friends in the art community he got some breaks. His name had been spread about and he didn't need to write a resume.' Where it counted, he was known for his work with both Fred M. Lamb and John Singer Sargent. His work as chief camouflage artist in the navy also lent presteige to his summary of experiences. He was in touch with his old friend Mr Lamb who would again be instrumental in helping him find work in his field. Much of what he had been doing was house painting or simple decorative work for buisness establishments. They were 'potboiler' jobs that kept food on the table but did nothing to stoke the fire that still burned in his belly for creative art work.

Lamb had welcomed Bob home and was delighted to meet his new wife and now his first child, Hannah, named after her grandmother who had brought her into the world. They were an extended family to the Lambs who delighted in the new baby as if it were their own grandchild. Mr Lamb very much wanted to find more creative work for his surrogate son.

Chapter 13

Spring arrived and Fred Lamb was called to accept an assignment for himself that he had done many times through the years. This was in Boston painting backdrops for theater productions. Such work lent itself to shared painting by two artists. Lamb had often asked Bob to help with this project from the time he had been his apprentice. He needed him again. He had more than he could handle and his several new young apprentice students were out of school and arriving daily for private art lessons. He had also built a reputaion as an outstanding portait painter and now that the ecomomy was picking up, he was beginning to get this kind of work again. He had a full plate and Bob's arrival was more than welcomed. Bob could work with him, as he had done in the past, on the theater drops and then Lamb would hand the job over to him to complete before the fall theater season began.

Bob gladly traded the broad house painters brush for the thin artist's brush and pallet and more creative work. He welcomed this project that required imagination and would take some length of time to complete. He also appreciated being able to catch the train home each night and be with his family.

Timing was everything and just as his theater drops were coming to completion he had the chance for a new assignment. A pastor of a small church in Boston needed restoration work on a mural in his church. This was just Bob's kind of work and he gladly took on the challenge of restoring a beautifully painted mural which was not too old, as the church had not been built that long ago. The pastor knew the original architect who now worked in New York City and was becoming very well known. When Bob completed the cleaning and restoration of the mural, the pastor was pleased with his work and suggested Bob talk with this architect for possibly getting more such work.

Dwight James Baum had become one of the outstanding architects in the country. He built churches, libraries, office buildings, and mansions through the eastern states and as far as Florida. The pastor, whose church mural Bob had restored, arranged for the two men to get together in New York. That meeting was the beginning of nearly twenty years of collaboration between the artist and architect.

Baum had an endless variety of jobs that kept Bob employed and challenged. When he didn't have work for him he loaned him to another architect who did have work. Several different men kept him constantly busy. Their work was varied from purely architectural decorating to complete mural painting. The one negative part to this was the distance he had to travel. The jobs were all over New York, in New Jersey, and one in Rhode Island. He was once sent to Florida.

The economic depression in the nation was still going on and expansion was slow. New construction was confined mostly to the east and big jobs were nearly all by architects working out of New York City. Bob Webb was making good money but suffering , along with his family, by their separation. He thought that if he didn't have to make train connections, and plan his life by train schedules, things would be better. The new automobiles seemed a perfect answer. He looked around and decided a truck would suit his purpose.   He bought a Ford Model 1920 Panel Truck; one of Fords first trucks.

This was Bob's first motor vehicle and he was so proud of it when he drove home he parked it in front of his parents house and honked the horn until everyone came out ! Rosa, with their lastest addition to the family, Thelma, and their first child Hannah, his mother and father all piled into the truck and he took them for a ride. Everyone and everything including ducks, goats, chickens, sheep scattered from the streets of Methuen! As he accelerated to twenty miles an hour his mother and his wife became so frightened they begged him to slow down.

Everyone was happy he had gotten the truck because this meant he could come home every weekend. He no longer needed to worry about leaving his ladder, and all his tools at the work sites. It had a single door on the back that could be locked. This still did not solve their problem of separation through the week however, and the strain was apparent on all members of his family.

His mother loved her grandchildren and spent much time with them, but she knew Rob should be home with his family through the week as well as the weekends. Neither she nor his father could fill that void. Rosa wished more than anything that one of these architects would have a job lasting longer than just a few weeks. They could then move to that location and think of building a house. Bob wrote letters home every night after a day of work, with all of them reading much the same. They expressed his loneliness and self-recrimination for what he had done or hadn't done the last time he was home.

The work kept coming in however, and he traveled unfinished roads, single lane dirt paths, and occasionally a concrete two lane highway. Most of his projects were in or near big cities in the east and he was able to travel on new connecting roads. Trucks were more common but cars were becoming a novelty for city dwellers. Baum always seemed able and ready to give Bob directions for how to get somewhere, and he often suggested the locations where he could stay while working. He, of course, had been to the locations and spent time there himself, having designed and built the structures. Sometimes he went with Bob or met him at a location to give him instructions as to what he wanted.

Mr. Lamb felt Bob might take advantage of where his latest work asignment was, in New York City, and study at a first rate art school. He suggested to him the Art Student League which offered free classses in the evenings. Bob was glad to take advantage of this and it helped fill the void of otherwise lonely evenings. He felt he gained something from these classes, while he was working on the Grand Central Station ceiling.

Bob's longest time away from home was an assignment in Tampa, Florida. He had been sent there previously for a short period of time but now Baum wanted him to stay for a matter of months. He had built a yacht club and wanted his artist to do all the decorative designs and wall paintings. When Bob arrived on the job he found that Baum had already sent a number of men ahead of him to help as he chose to use them. They were laborers with a degree of skills that were helpful, plus the fact they did 'grunt' work he didn't want to spend time doing such as erecting scaffolding, moving and storing furniture, and cleaning up after the job was done.

These were mostly immigrants from Italy who apparently did nothing but travel the country and freelance their skills where ever needed. After this job, they began to show up on sites where Bob was sent. Mr. Baum always paid them himself. These men knew ahead of time what was expected of them and they would arrive and begin their work. This made it much easier for the architects artist-decorator. Some had limited artistic skills brought with them from the old country. Bob quickly learned he could use them in a variety of ways and depend on them.

While in Florida, he took time to look around and find out what was going on in the way of construction. It was not surprising that many people were coming to Florida to live. He found his skills to be in great demand here and was confident that, if he were to bring his family to Florida, there would be plenty of work. This would be the kind of decorating and painting of murals that he had been trained to do. He would talk it over with Rosie when he got home and see if she too thought it a good idea to move. He would not be giving up working for Mr. Baum but would have access to many more architects who were busy in this state. Baum had always loaned him out to other architects anyway.

Baum had been hinting that he had a big project he was working on in Florida and if Bob wanted it he would have to relocate his family. He stated this was something that would take a very long time to complete. Bob thought he might 'jump the gun' and arrive early and be here when Baum wanted him. Architects seemed to pass him around and he really worked for everyone. His mind was made up; he would bring his family to Florida.

Chapter 14

Arriving back in New York, he first went to Baum's office to check in, as he always did, and collect his pay as well as get a new assignment. Bob mentioned to Baum his thought of moving to Florida and his boss gave him his blessing. The architect expressed that he only had one or two constructions left to finish in the east. He wanted Bob to work on them but he could leave when he was ready. Baum gave him no specific idea of what he was building in Florida. He would simply say it was a big project and he would need him to be there later on.

He let it be known however, that Bob, his artist-decorator, was his man and he would expect him to be available for work when Baum wanted him. He paid very well and the jobs were varied and interesting. This was no problem for Bob knowing he had to be flexible. This kind of work would always require travel and time away from home. With the nation being in a depression he knew he was lucky to have work. He and Rosa would continue to dream of his getting a job that would last for years, so that they might stay in one place and establish a home and roots. The Florida project might be the one.

Baum had always seen to it that Bob was never out of work. He gave him the name of an architect to look up when he got to Florida. This man was well known and doing a lot of work in both east and west Florida. Baum was sure that he would have decorative work for Bob. Baum again stated that his next project was one that would be of long duration and that Bob should not think of any job he might get as being permanent. He would expect him to be ready to go to work immediately.

Back home, in learning of Florida, Rosa felt their dream had come true for settling in a place where they could put down roots. Bob was grateful to his parents, particularly his mother, who had not only acted as midwife again, for the new baby Thelma, who had just been delivered before he left, but for her help with much that was required in a family with young children.

Bob was profuse in his appreciation of her but his mother dismissed him, expressing her delight in being a grandmother. Being able to help was a part of it.

Bob's wife and children were all that remained at the homestead and both his parents looked forward to their visiting each day. Bob's brothers and sister Jane were already in Florida, having moved there with their spouses and children in recent years.

Bob and Rosa tentatively made plans for their move. Houses and public buildings were going up rapidly in Florida and they would be there at the beginning of the building boom. The one big factor holding them in Massachusetts was his parents. He could not think of leaving them on this remote farm alone, especially with winter coming on. Bob, and Jane particularly, had been trying to persuade them to sell out and move to Florida. This was no lifestyle for an elderly couple. Their farmhouse had not been modernized, they did not drive a motor car, and they simply missed their children.

Jane would help them get settled. She had a good nursing job and was about to start her own nursing home for the elderly. Years after their mother's death, Robert Sr. would come to live in her new establishment and spend the rest of his life there. Bob told of going to visit his father. He said he always took along a bottle of scotch and the two would share it. His father was not allowed to drink alcohal on the premises and looked forward to his son's visits. Bob discreetly left a little with him that he might enjoy latter.

Robert Sr. is suppose not to have gotten along well with the nurses at his daughter's nursing home and played many nasty tricks on them. It seems he resented having to follow a routine and take orders from the 'women in white.' His mind was keen and his energy took him on nightly walks outside the grounds. He told his son he had found a pub where he enjoyed spending time. He would sneak out and back into his room in the middle of the night. This went on almost up to his death at age ninty-nine ! His daughter was nor fooled and would routinely send an aid out to escort him back home. Bob, Jr. always said his father lived to be one hundred but Thelma and Hannah disputed this.

Here, much younger, and still on the family farm, Robert Senior was aware of his situation. He thought he was being of help to his names sake by being present for support of his daughter-in-law and his grandchildren when Bob was out of town. He thought however, that he should encourage his son to make a move. He decided to tell Rob of his search for a buyer to the property. At the barbershop a man from the city, a buisness man he knew, casually asked him if he would ever consider selling what he had! Robert hadn't seriously thought of it until then.

He loved his grandchildren who gave him laughter, of which there was very little lately, however he did have his wife and himself to think about. He was tired of caring for the property and dealing with tenants who, of late, could hardly pay their rents. His boys were gone and not interested in the farm. They had helped him when they were youngsters but now he had it all to do himself and he was no longer young. He listened, over a cup of tea, as his wife read the latest letter from their daughter discribing Florida. Hannah had kept the fire in the kitchen stove going until he got home--it was the only source of heat in the house-and it was cozy and comfortable but not adequate when the Massachusetts winter unleashed its fury.

Jane's letters were very persuasive. He could hardly believe there was such a place where it was summer all the time! He would ask that buisnessman in the barbershop if he was interested in buying his property. Not long after these kitchen musings Robert Senior had no trouble selling the farm and rental properties.

When Bob got home from where he had been working in New Jersey and learned of his father's decision, he said that settled it for him as well. He and Rosa had already made tentative plans for moving to Florida and it seemed providential that his parents should also have the chance to sell out and seek a better climate.

Jane would help them get settled. Bob would help them on this end. He would first take time to assist his mentor, Mr. Lamb, in completing a drop curtain for the Boston Conservatory and some theatre drops he had started. They would work together out of Lamb's new barn studio in Stoughton and carry the finished work to Boston. Next he would take a couple of weeks to help his father wrap up buisness and make the transfer of his property to the new owner. It was a sad feeling when it was all completed and his parents left. Bob had grown up on this land and it held many memories; mostly good. But it was time to leave.

He and Rosa had very few possessions. He had hoped to keep the camouflage drawings from his navy days, but had been surprised some weeks earlier when two uniformed men came to the door and asked for the navy ship drawings he had. They claimed them as U.S.Government property. There would be no questions or problems, they said, if Webb simply handed them over. Bob knew there were duplicates of these at the navy base, but he said nothing.

On reflection he knew he probably shouldn't have taken the originals. He might have taken the duplicates, but he was the artist and had a possessive feeling about his work. No one could fight the navy, however. He went to the trunk where they were kept and pulled them out and handed them over to these two big, tough looking, men in uniform. He asked no questions of them and doubted he would have gotten an answer.

Chapter 15

The truck was loaded first with all the tools he would need for his work; paints, brushes, pots, and buckets, an extension ladder, ground cloths, his tool box. Next came summer clothes, bedding, and finally the children's toys to keep them happy for the long drive. Hannah, the oldest, went into the back and the door was cracked open a bit for light and air and made secure. Rosa would hold the baby Thelma, on her lap. Rosa had assembled food enough to last for at least a few days of the trip. By the time they got further south they figured to be able to get fresh produce or eat in the many guest houses having sprung up along the new highways. Water, showers and toilets. with changing tables for babies, were available at many service pump stations where gasoline was sold.

Bob stood for a long while looking past his mother's kitchen garden now picked clean and with the ground turned over. He looked down to the cattle barn and smiled, remembering the time he rigged up a pully from his bedroom window to the barn. He fixed it so he could pull a rope and cause buckets of feed to spill over into the animals troughs, thus saving himself from having to get up early in the morning and go out in the cold to feed them. His father didn't see the genius of the idea and threatened him with a thrashing if he didn't disassemble his device immediately. It bothered him most that he wasn't allowed to see if it might ever have worked! He had to laugh that his father called him lazy for trying to invent a labor saving device. Men were doing it all the time in this 'modern' age of inventions he was now a part of.

He looked at the chicken yard and tears came to his eyes as he recalled the tragedy that happened there years earlier when he was a little boy. He wondered what was wrong with him that he should think of this after so long a time. It was then that Rosa walked up behind him and put her arms around his waist. He turned and she kissed his tear streaked cheek. It was all right. Everything would be all right from now on. He vowed he would never be separated from her again. Florida would give him enough work to hold him there. They got into the truck, Bob made a joke about their being gypsys, and they drove off.

His parents and siblings were already in Florida and looking forward to their arrival. His father had concern the truck might not make it all the way. The senior Webbs took the train and were met by their youngest, Arthur, in his new automobile. They knew Robert could think of a variety of ways of getting there having told them of a few. Bob said he might just take his time and work his way down. The truck was filled with what he would need to paint a house or decorate a building. He even had his advertising that went with him! When he first bought his truck he painted a logo on the side, "Bob Webb--Painting and Decorating" and a picture of an artists palette.

Traveling and discovering America in the new auto machines was the vacation of envy in the 1920's. People just took off and went somewhere, often camping beside the road. Bob would have made a fun adventure of it. With money he had saved and time, they may have preferred to stay in the many guest houses that were springing up at gas pump sites along the main routes. These 'super-highways' were little more than dirt roads and it took adventurous spirits to travel interstate for long distances.

Whatever he did and however long it took is not known. We know they got there, as he reported the whole family jubulantly gathering to meet them upon arrival. All the ruckus, by the family, made the difficulties of the trip, with an infant and young child, worthwhile. The senior Webbs, sister Jane and younger brother Arthur, and their spouses and childtren, welcomed them and made them comfortable. The whole Webb clan had now assembled in Florida. All but one of the older brothers made Florida their home. That brother had been injured in the war and spent the rest of his life in a veterans home.

Another brother, was later tragically killed by an unbalanced convict recently released from prison. In seeking revenge he mistook the young Webb as his enemy. This nearly killed their mother. It helped that the rest of her children and grandchildren were with her in Florida.

Four Webb brothers had all been in some branch of the service during the First World War. Arthur had been the exception, having been too young to enlist. To make up for this, when the Second World War came along, he decided to enlist in the army engineer corps. He and his four sons were all good auto mechanics and the millitary needed mechanics. They all enlisted together and were assigned to the same base throughout their time of enlistment. Arthur claims to have negotiated this arrangement telling the recruiting officer he would bring all of his sons in to enlist together if they could stay together. Bob bypassed this war, being just above the age limit, and with family responsibilities.

A shared adventure of the two youngest brothers, during their early days in Florida, involved alligators! Arthur had already begun hunting the reptiles for their skins. The hides were a very lucrative business at that time. Bob said he went out with Arthur once at night but would never do it again. Arthur was not afraid to go over the side of a boat after a big thrashing gator! He could bind the jaws and the two of them would haul the gator into the boat!

Bob had enough of this, as did Arthur, in a very short time. Both men lived to an old age with each following his own interests. Arthur tried many ventures and developed a skill for investing in the stock market and later became wealthy. The brothers drifted apart, as much by seperate interests, and finally by geography, as anything.

Bob knew he was in Florida for a special purpose and he remained single minded to that pursuit. Something big was about to happen that would give him the chance of his lifetime. This is the way his architect boss discribed it and he would wait for Baum to come to Florida and tell him what it was. He could be patient and fill his time with other art work. There was plenty of decorating everywhere to be done.

Chapter 16

*B*ob had no trouble finding decorating jobs in Florida in the 1920's. When D.J. Baum encouraged him to go to Florida he had given him the name of Addison Mizner to contact for employment. Mizner was an eccentric but brilliant architect who walked round in his pajamas most of the day with a monkey on his shoulder. He needed an artist and hired Bob immediately. Bob liked working for him and appreciated that, after assigning him a job, he didn't bother him again until the work was finished. Baum had told him in New York that he would be coming down later and would have a big, long term, assignment for him. He worked several months for Mizner before his New York boss showed up.

While on a ladder one day, Bob heard his

name being called and looked down to see Baum waving at him. He was shouting, "Get on down here Webb, I've got a big job for you to do." He told him he could finish what he was doing but that he, Baum, had a claim on him. Baum reminded Mizner that he had only loaned his decorator to him temporarily and now he wanted him back. He had an important job that he felt only Webb could do. That would be the decorating of Ca'd'Zan, the John and Mable Ringling mansion in Sarasota.

Mizner reluctantly said goodbye to Bob and told him if he ever needed work he knew where he could find him. Mizner and Bob would work together one more time before the Webbs left permanently for the north. That would be years down the road, however, and for now Bob would go with Baum to meet his new boss, John Ringling.

Ringling, the famous circus magnate, had an office in downtown Sarasota where the two men went. John Ringling greeted them with a warm handshake, after transfering his ever present cigar from one hand to the other. He was a tall, robust man with a direct and engaging manner. Bob immediately liked him and knew he had met a man he would never forget. He sensed an inner strength and uncompromising power in Ringling.

The young artist came to have great respect for the circus man and would emmulate him in many ways throughout his life. He wished to identify with him not only in his work ethic but his character. He was a gentleman with warmth and humanity. The two immediately came to know they had much in common; especially in their shared passion for work and the boundless energy to get it done.

More than a home, Ca'd'Zan was an impressive mansion in the style of an Italian Renaissance palace. Baum had designed and carried out its construction over the past year. The construction was nearly complete; although there seemed no end to it. John and Mable Ringling continually thought of new additions they wanted. Baum wisely stopped adding at a certain point knowing that Ringling, although wealthy in talk, was sometimes limited in the check book. There were times when he had millions but other times, when weather was bad, and the circus couldn't get out, he went broke.

Bob's job would be to paint murals and decorative designs on the walls and ceilings of the various rooms, hallways, bedrooms, and all public and private quarters of the mansion. He would be responsible for carved and painted motifs on the woodwork and the furniture.

This was an assignment that would take years to complete.

He was twenty-five years old when first starting the project. It wasn't long before he was put in charge of all the decorating at Ca'd Zan, which in Italian means "House of John." Bob needed living arrangements for his wife and children and Ringling gave him his own garage on the grounds that, with a few adjustments, was made livable for the young family.

Baum had hired the decorator-\artist, Webb, for this job but continually kept him busy elsewhere. Bob felt that he was in a three-ring circus, literally, with so much work to do. The architect's office in Sarasota was turning out drawings for churches, yacht clubs, municipal buildings, hotels and residences. Baum was sending Webb all over west Florida to start the decorating on these projects. It was Mable Ringling who called a halt to all this extra work and made a total claim on his time. This was her mansion, and she knew what she wanted, and it was her wish to have Bob Webb get it done. Her collection of photos and prints from Italy would show him just how she wanted it. From then on, he became chief decorator and answerable only to the Ringlings, and Mable Ringling in particular. He saw very little of Baum after that.

Incredibly, on the first day of work, the men who had worked with him in New York and New Jersey, and at the yacht club in Tampa, showed up ready to be assigned a job! Baum had sent them over. They were the same Italian immigrants who had first come to Baum in New York bringing their skills learned in the old country. Their ability to decorate architecture was unique and Bob found them to be invaluable. In years to come, these men would follow him to various job sites, often beginning work before he even arrived.

Though still in his twenties, Robert Webb had experience and training and a quality of leadership that invited men to want to work with him. He was demanding yet clear in his expectations. These, mostly Italian immigrants, knew so well what was required in being helpers to a master decorator of churches and public buildings they hardly needed telling. They were men who, like Bob, loved the work and needed the money. Some would bring their wives and children,who had skills that could be used such as making flowers of clay and patterns to be applied to the various architectural forms. It was a happy atmosphere with everyone busy and involved in what they were doing.

Terracotta was used extensively at Ca'd Zan,

thus cutting cost to about a tenth over stone, which was the first material Baum had planned to use. Ringling's finances required the change, though they were just as happy with the results by using clay. Molds were made for the decorative surrounds of doors and windows and other Venetian gothic motifs with most of this work being done by the women and children.

Mrs. Ringling loved Italians and was delighted by this totally engaged work force. They responded to her and loved her as all who knew her did. Bob said she was a lovely person and he appreciated her energy and intelligence. He said she was beautiful and vivacious and had a gift for visualizing an idea and projecting it to the workers. She knew what she wanted and, importantly, could tell him or show him pictures from Italy. Their objective was to partially duplicate the Doge's Palace in Venice, which also had a gondola landing, as Ca'd Zan came to have.

When the Ringlings were not having a party, after the gondola landing was completed, they would put a roll of music on their player organ and get into the gondola to enjoy it. The music was so loud it could be heard across the water. Mrs. Ringling also had pet exotic birds that would fly out over the water and return through the open doors to perch on chandeliers or wherever they fancied. They never seemed to want to fly away permanently.

Bob's regard for Mr. Ringling was a young man's adulation. He admired his generousity and the care he showed for his circus people as well as his animals. Ringling said that if animals were fed well, they would never be aggressive toward people. To prove his point he would frequently walk alone and unarmed into the cage of his giant gorilla, Gargantua. He would talk to her, give her a banana and back out of the cage. One day the keeper of Gargantua came to Mr. Ringling and reported that the gorilla was unhappy and very restless. He felt that something was wrong but didn't know what it was. She had recently been moved to a new cage.

Mr. Ringling went with the keeper to check her out. She was pacing her cage and wiping her brow first with her right paw and then the left. On seeing them she retreated to a back corner of her cage. She then turned and ran straight toward Ringling, stopping directly in front of him. She jumped up and down as if to tell him to do something about the situation. He understood her and turning to the keeper said, "I know what's wrong with her. She has to go to the bathroom. Would you want to do that in front of everyone?"

In giving her a new cage, they had neglected to hang her privacy curtain at the back right corner. She was modest! The workers proceed to find a shower curtain and hung it as it had been before. They added a hairbrush and mirror she liked to play with, and the problem was solved.

Chapter 17

*R*ingling respected the fact that his animals were wild. He never did anything foolish and wouldn't allow any laxity in safety with his workers. He had learned that with humane treatment and good food, they could be managed. From a circus family of parents and brothers before him, he knew the business well. Nevertheless, Bob, and especially Rosa, had some misgivings about the animals that were let out to pasture together. The winter months went by fast, however, and the whole menangiere was soon boarded in their individual cages and onto the circus train in which the Ringlings had there own private car. This railroad company had brought their tracks onto the Ringling property so that the animals could easily be loaded. They were then off to the East and the Midwest to perform in the small towns and big cities of the nation.

A dapper dresser, with bowler hat, cuff links and coordinated colors, Ringling carried (or "wore" as the English, and Bob Webb, would say) a cane, and he frequently wore spats on his shoes. He loved to party and would entertain lavishly till all hours of the night. Celebrity people in the nation from politics, sports, entertainment, business and industry were invited. Although it was the prohibition era, booze never stopped flowing at the Ringling parties. Bob said that a boat regularly came to the docking station at night and unloaded cases of the best alcoholic drinks money could buy. It was locked away in a secret place in the mansion. Bob had been given the key however, and sometimes the temptation was great. He was free to come and go as he pleased and Ringling said he had a standing invitation to their many parties.

One night Bob had planned to stay home when there was a knock on the screen door. He peered out and down and there stood Tiny Tim, the circus midget, breathing heavily. He said that Mr. Ringling needed Webb at the party right away. It seemed that Will Rogers was a guest and would entertain if he had a partner who would act as his straight-man.

Tim didn't wait for an answer. He was told to hurry and he turned and ran as fast as possible. No wonder he was so winded. If his boss told him to hurry, he knew it would take him three times longer than a man three times his height. He shouted over his shoulder, as he ran, that Bob was to wear his work clothes.

Bob met Rogers, who briefly told him what to do and shoved him out onto the stage. Rogers was a master at rope tricks, as well as being an actor. He had Bob hold a lit candle and with a flick of the rope some twenty feet away he knocked the flame out, leaving the smoking candle in Bob's hand. After several such tricks and story telling, which he was good at, he whispered to Bob to stay on the stage while he, Rogers, would leave!

Rogers then lassoed him. Bob saw the rope drop down around him to his ankles and felt it quickly tighten. He felt the pull and a jerk and began to teeter. Being young and agile and used to climbing ladders and bending in all directions, he put on quite a contorted act before falling to the floor. Not knowing what was happening, it didn't require any acting on his part to look startled. Will dragged him off the stage and the audience couldn't stop laughing. After being released, the two took a curtain call in which Rogers led Bob into a shuffle dance to end the show. Rogers was a loved homespun philosopher, as well as actor and rope man. His picture hung in many homes throughout the nation. It was a memorable performance for Bob, and one he would never forget.

Ringling seldom involved himself in the day to day operations of getting a job done that others were doing for him. Indeed, he kept strange hours. He had gotten used to working in the middle of the night when out on the road with the circus. The tents had to go up in the predawn hours and come down when the rest of the world was sleeping. There were times, however when they couldn't go anywhere. Ringling sometimes went broke when rain and mud, and ice and snow, kept them from moving. When they couldn't get the circus out they made no money.

The situation was so desperate at one point that Ringling couldn't pay his people or feed them or the animals. He called a meeting and explained the situation to everyone and told them they could leave if they liked. They could try to go out and get employment in the community and come back when he could pay them again. They all said they would stay and make do with what they had until things got better. Besides, where could the fat lady, the midget and all the rest, trained only for the circus, go? They were not just loyal because they had to be however, they genuinely loved their employer and would do anything for him.

The meat packing company, upon learning of their plight, continued sending meat for the animals, which was used as well to feed the troops. They told Ringling he didn't have to pay them back; it was a gift. The trains that carried them to the Midwest, and further, carried them, at no charge, till they were able to make money. Loaded and still on the estate, the trainers slept on top the boxcars, until the weather looked to be turning and they could go. The benefactors who kept the circus alive and moving felt that the show had to go on. The circus was "the greatest show on earth" at that time. The country needed it, and couldn't get along without it.

Mable and John Ringling often went to Italy in search of motifs for their mansion. They incidentally also began to collect paintings which later comprised the nucleus of the museum they would leave to the City of Sarasota, Mrs. Ringling would bring pictures of palaces, scenes of Venice, detailed sketches of moldings, cornices, columns, murals, windows, and doors. She also brought expensive cameo jewelry back with her.

One day when she was trying to decide what design to put in the ceiling she went to her bedroom and brought back a tray full of cameo jewelry. She laid it down in front of Bob and told him to use these as designs for the ceiling. He took them up on the ladder with him and laid them out on the scaffolding. They stayed there, and he copied them for several months until the ceiling was completed.

Chapter 18

The circus people lived in close quarters and shared their lives together. Sarasota was their winter home, and they lived in their trailers or wagons on the grounds of the Ringling estate. Incredible as it seems, and as stated a concern to Bob and Rosa, through these winter months the wild animals were all turned out to graze together in a large, fence-enclosed pasture next to the living area of the performers, the garage where the Webbs lived, and Ringling's own residence! According to Bob, each species of animal took a corner or location on the grounds as their own. Elephants, tigers, lions, and giraffs all grazed within the same enclosure without fighting or posing a threat to one another or their human neighbors.

The only threat from the wild that occurred was after Mrs. Ringling had sand delivered for Bob's children to play in. One day, when Bob went to check on them, he saw a large rattlesnake sunning himself, not ten feet from the girls. They didn't seem to have noticed it! Bob ran to the garage and got a hoe and killed the snake. He told Mrs Ringling about the incident and she immediately had a safe enclosure built in the yard so that nothing could get to the children in the future. Nothing could keep out mosquitoes, however.

Florida was still much of a jungle and disease carrying mosquitoes were prevelant. Rosa was bitten and contracted a kind of nerve disorder that she would have for the rest of her life. Bob took this very hard and blamed himself. He could never forgive himself for bringing her into such an environment. She became quite incapacitated, requiring round the clock attention. Bob looked after her and the children as best he could while continuing to work for Ringling.

Finding the help his wife needed and wanted was difficult. She was from the South, born and bred, and brought up to believe that only colored women could be housekeepers and care for the sick. Black help just couldn't be found in Sarasota at that time, and so he did all the work himself. Years went by and life went on pretty much as before. Bob was anxious to get his mansion work done however, and leave Florida, though he enjoyed what he was doing and liked the circus people.

After dinner one day, he took one of his frequent walks through the circus compound. It carried him beneath the palm trees to the sound of a calliope. There, in a row of wagons, the performers and workers lived. He heard his name being called in a high pitched, little person octave, and turned to see that it was Tiny Tim! They had met at breakfast earlier that day on the rare time Bob came to eat with the circus people. Bob had liked the little man when he first met him. He was all of twenty-two inches tall, and a perfectly proportioned miniature of a man. "Come meet my wife," Tim shouted. "All three hundred pounds and acres and acres of her and she's all mine." He jumped on the lap of the 'fat lady' of the circus and climbed up her arm and seated himself on her shoulder. She was jolly, and laughed. Tim said they had been married a short time before Bob had arrived. Bob didn't know whether he was serious or not!

He congratulated the little man and wished his wife much happiness. They exchanged news of the day and Bob confirmed again how wonderful married life was and said he had to hurry home to his own sweetheart. On the way a trapeze artist was turning summersaults in the yard and the strong man was lifting weights, the clowns were being funny even with their make-up off. He decided that he liked it here and he liked these people. They were genuine and would do anything in the world for a person, but especially for the Ringlings. Bob saw no reason to share his own problems with them however; they seemed to have plenty of their own. He suspected they knew of his wife's illness anyway, and felt that sympathy was not what he needed. That was true. What he needed was more hours in the day and more hands to help.

The routine for Bob was difficult but not impossible. He was adjusting to his new role as housekeeper, nurse, child care giver, cook and 'chief bottle washer,' as the saying goes. He met his men each morning after first having a conference with Mrs. Ringling. Everyone knew their jobs, including himself, and could proceed in organized harmony. He frequently went home to check on his wife and children. Rosa would sometimes fall on the floor and had to be helped up. Mabel Ringling knew of her condition and was very supportive. She had recently been diagnosed with diabetes herself and could empathize. Sadly she would live only one more year to enjoy her mansion home after it's completion.

Chapter 19

Ca'dZan was Baum's architectural triumph. Structurally beautiful, as a mansion should be, it also was exquisite in detail. The high ceiling of the Great Hall had skylights surrounded by panels which were covered with a wood called 'pecky cypress.' This wood cannot be found today; all that was available has been taken from the waters, where it had been buried for years, on the east coast of Florida. It was uniquely grooved on the surface and was full of tiny holes from bug and worm infestation. It had deep ridges and a reddish color that gave it a special quality. Although a beautiful wood, it was hard to work with. To cut or saw it was extremely difficult, and to paint over it nearly impossible. However, it was painted and designs were put on it. It was used to make beams, as well as panels in the frieze work above the balcony columns. Some pieces of furniture can be found with it as a decorative addition.

As a covered court, the Great Hall was most impressive. It had a balcony on three sides held up by columns, which gave access to the private guest rooms. French tapestries hung above and over the balustrade and on the walls across alcoves. The ceiling panels took on the decorative motifs of the Italian jewelry Mrs. Ringling had brought out on a tray and given to Bob to paint from. In a repeat pattern he added his own designs to that of the cameos. Everything was done in freehand painting with the exception of stencil work required for beams.

These stencils were drawn freehand from color plates Bob had of the walls and ceiling of the Davanzati Palace in Florence. He had found these plates years earlier at a bookstore sale in New York City. He bought them just because he liked them. They were similar to some of the decorative work he now inherited from his predecessor, who had started the work at Ca'd Zan before he arrived. That was Leon Buechler, a man in his sixties when he turned the work over to the young twenty-five year old. The height of the ceiling and scaffolding required to reach one's work was in itself daunting. Robert Webb loved the challenge. He loved the Renaissance period from which this work drew its inspiration.

Bob said he never made designs ahead of time, but just started painting-- that was how the Italians did it. His stencil work, of course, had to fit a space on beams and occasionally columns. He worked freehand from his own sketches done from the cameos or plates. Another artist, Willy Pogany, painted the ceiling in the recreation room. Bob did the decorative work using twenty-three karat gold leaf on the grafette.

He and Pogany frequently worked together in the Sarasota area before and briefly after the Ringling project was completed. They decorated a large hotel in Sarasota, the El Vernona. Bob considered this one of his most outstanding works. It was rich with color and he was proud of what he had been able to do there. "I'm not sure I could ever get those colors of the El Vernona again" he commented when talking about the hotel.

Some seven years had gone by and when winter came the Ringlings took off for Europe as they frequently did in the northern cold, wet months. Bob had detailed instructions as to what he was to have finished by the time they returned. He had been on the job nonstop these many years. They were delighted with what he had done, however John Ringling was running out of money and had begun to cut corners on his ambitions for the decorating as well as architectural additions he wanted.

In later years, Bob would point out where he had to shortcut on completing a small area of the ceiling because Ringling had told him it was finished. He had covered the area so as to give it a vignette conclusion and not to appear as a blank space. Ringling couldn't go on for lack of funds, but it really was finished by Bob's estimate of what their goals had been. He had met Mabel's expectations, as well as his own. His architect employer D.J. Baum, was happy with it and ready to call it quits. Indeed it was Baum who had been instrumental in halting all activities. He was the designer and builder of Ca'd Zan and he paid the bills. Ringling was no longer paying him thus the job had to be finished. After seven years Baum now had other work in mind for his artist-decorator.

Dwight J. Baum divided his time between his offices in Sarasota and New York. He had plenty of work to do in a variety of places. First, he wanted Bob to go to east Florida to work on a church. A Baptist Church there needed interior restoration of the wall paintings and other decorative additions in the sanctuary. Baum trusted that his artist would know what to do.

His crew of Italian workers had gone ahead and would prepare the church. They would erect the scaffolding, lay out ground cloths, paint a base coat where needed and make repairs. Bob would wrap up things at Ca'd Zan, which meant cleaning his work areas, gathering up tools, checking things out one last time. He would take care of his familys business. Baum had left him in charge of locking up where necessary as the Ringlings were not in residence. He told him there was no hurry; his family could stay as long as was neccessary before making a more permanent move to New Jersey, their next destination.

Housekeepers were more available at that time and the Webbs had one they were satisfied with. Bob was able to leave his family for the time spent with the Baptist church and later in New York and New Jersey. His wife had adjusted to her condition so that she did not require such close attention. His parents, brothers and sister were still in Florida and they frequently visited the young family and could check up on them in his absence. His sister, a nurse, was happy to do so. Bob felt fortunate in having been close to his family in Florida for better than seven years. New Jersey looked promising as another place of long duration where he would be at home all the time.

Meanwhile, he had a job yet to do here in Florida. The Baptist church was waiting for him. He arrived at the church several days later than he had planned. To his dismay, and chagrin, his men were well into the work. Indeed, they had the most visible, up front part of a wall and ceiling painted. Cupids drifted through fluffy clouds, a Madonna was stepping through something that looked like a quarter of the moon, stars glittered throughout. Bob was flabbergasted! All he could do was shake his head and take a deep breath.

These men were all Catholics, and to them this was what a church should look like. To a Protestant Baptist, these symbols of faith had no place in their worship. What to do? They had used up all the funds to buy paints, gold leaf – which was and is extremely expensive – and their time which was expensive as well. The church was really quite beautiful. Bob had them continue but delete what he thought would raise theological debate. What they had already done was done, however. They didn't have the time or money to do it over. He decided to leave it. When the men were finished, they left town in a hurry, already having been paid by their architect boss.

Bob learned later that the congregation of the church was so divided about how they felt that the conflict caused the church to split. Henceforth, he claimed, it was known as the "Divided Baptist Church."

Returning to his garage home on the Ringling estate, Bob was aware that his family couldn't stay here much longer. Baum had told him of another Baptist church in Montclair, New Jersey. He wanted him and Lamb, Bob's old teacher, to work together on painting murals and decorating the church. It meant ongoing work and an income and he would like working with Lamb again. Baum wanted to see him in his New York office "soon" and he had said " yes" he would be there.

To drive to New York would be a long and even dangerous trip in bad weather. Bob remembered other trips and decided instead to opt for taking the train. He wanted to visit his brother on the east coast of Florida and was sure of catching a train over there. The Seaboards Air Line Railroad ran near where Arthur lived and he could leave his panel truck for him to use and retrieve it again upon returning. In discusing the trip with Rosie, she thought taking the train a good idea suggesting that driving was too risky. Perhaps she was remembering their trip to Florida some seven years earlier. Roads were probably better now but the weather had not changed and could make a trip hazardous.

Baum had no more work for him in Florida, and even if he did, the family would still have to find living quarters. The building boom had crested and tapered off and without Baum's assignments, there would be little work. Also a great depression had hit the nation. The frequent projects Bob could get on his own would not produce a regular income and " keep the family in shoes," as he said. It seemed to be his lot in life, and the way of an artist-decorator, to keep moving around. The pay was good, when there was work, and he had saved money. He and Rosie wanted a home, and he had saved enough to buy an acre of ground and put a house on it. They dreamed, that with his next work place, they could do just that.

At one time in Florida, they had bought a house and furnished it, but lost it immediately to the bank; just as so many others had lost theirs after the stock market crash. He owed very little, but the bank wouldn't wait or make a new arrangement with him. It was business, they had said. It was his beautiful, waterfront home they wanted as he saw it. The next time he'd be smarter. But he decided there would be no next time. If he couldn't pay cash for something, he just wouldn't buy it. And that's what he did for the rest of his life! He never went into debt for anything again. Now, there was something new to look forward to and no point in looking back. A lesson had been learned and his family was still in their garage home on the Ringling estate.

Chapter 20

*B*read baking was something Bob enjoyed and with one day left before leaving for the east coast, he proceeded to bake four loaves of bread. One would go to his brother, and one he would keep for himself to eat on the train, along with a wedge of cheese. While the bread was rising, he mopped the floor. While the loaves were baking, he did a laundry and hung it outside on the children's enclosure fence to dry. When the bread was baked, it was time for the family to sit down together and have hot bread with molasses and bean soup he had made the day before. Family shopping was very important so that the pantry would be loaded up before he left. He saved the shopping trip for last.

On the way home from the market, he picked

up Rosa's aid-companion at the bus station where she came in from the little rural black community outside of Sarasota. She told him she had arranged for a ride every day while he was gone. She could now stay on the job as long as they needed her. Bob had arranged for family members to be there but now he would just ask his sister, Jane , to stay the nights. She would be a support and relief to the aid-companion. He left enough money with Rosa to pay their bills. Not knowing how long he would be gone, more could be sent as needed. The phone Baum had put in the mansion, would come in handy for them to communicate. He had permission to use it at any time to check on the family.

With his suitcase in hand, he picked up his lunch bag and the extra loaf of bread, and tossed them into the back of the truck. The children pulled him into a tag game and he chased with them until they dropped. Finally kissing his family goodbye he drove out past the mansion, down the road, and across the railroad tracks to the highway east. It was still early in the day when he left for his brother's house across the state. It usually rained in the afternoons this time of year, and with only a two hour drive ahead he would miss the rain. Not knowing the train schedule he was yet confident there would be one leaving once or twice daily for New York City. Arthur needed his truck and Bob was glad to have him keep it while he was gone. He was an especially good mechanic and Bob knew he would return it in better condition than when he got it.

It was raining when he boarded the train and the decision not to drive proved a good one. He threw his overnight bag into the rack above and laid the sack with his lunch in it on the seat beside him. The car was not full and there was plenty of room to stretch out his long frame. This was a good time to reflect on where he had been and where he was going in his life. Trains had carried him to new jobs, the Navy, art shows, and even to church with his mother as a little boy and now to another new life in the north. Thankfully, New Jersey didn't get as cold as Massachusetts. Maybe the doctors there could help his wife, and his children would have good schools to go to. They all might even like to go to the church together ! Rosie might like the one he was decorating and he wouldn't be hearing her pestering him all the time to go to church with her.

After a time, the weather cleared some and the landscape took on a foggy mist drifting over fields and far off trees that followed streams. There were many cattle now grazing on wide open pastures. They were still in Florida, but he had never thought of ranches being here. Where did the cattle go at night? He saw no big red barns. It was definately a different landscape than in the north.

His thoughts drifted to the house he wanted to build. It could be done on weekends and at night, if lighting could be rigged up. If they only got to live in it a few years before having to move again, their life would be improved. It would be their home on their own plot of ground. He would make it happen. Each new job was always a challenge and exciting for being different, yet nothing he had done so far had been exhausting to him. Never without energy and now with the money, he would make the time to build it. The men he had known who had accomplished anything just stepped up and "did it."

That Baptist church debacle was a fluke he wouldn't let happen again. His men had never gone so far ahead of his orders before. He would make sure of a better rein on them if they worked for him again. They were good men, but limited when it came to making judgments about anything. He would treat them as he had learned to do with those assigned to him in the Navy. It had been good training, and perhaps what they needed from him was clearer and firmer directions. In the future he would tell them exactly what he wanted and then hold them to following his orders.

Baum hadn't said anything about that Baptist Church job in their recent telephone conversation. Baum had a phone put in the Ringling Mansion when he was working there and needed to call back to his office in New York. Now he used it to talk to Bob and, had also given Bob permission to use it.   Maybe the pastor or church board hadn't complained. He would forget it himself; put it away somewhere like a canceled check. His thoughts drifted as the mist and "money" came into focus.

Money was always something to think about. Like Ringling, it was probably always best to act like he had a lot of money; people respect you more. They have no respect for those who have nothing, and act like it. He would work to establish this illusion over the years. He didn't care about becoming wealthy but his family needed security. In later years, following Ringlings example he learned that claiming to have wealth also gave him power.   Bob was never without money nor was he greedy, nor did he flount what he did have. He was frugal and always had goals thus he had something to save for. He became very good at saving, examining carefully every minute outlay of the smallest denomination. If he could wait for a week or a month or a year and still needed or wanted a thing then the money would be spent for it. He was tight! Yet he spent lavishly when the time came to realize the goal he had saved for.

The conductor came through asking for their tickets. He had left the door open between cars, and the cooler air rushing through roused everyone from their reveries. Bob gave him his ticket and got out his bread and cheese. He had sliced the bread at home and cut the cheese into squares. Water from his thermos was still cold. A Florida orange in the sack was Rosie's contribution. It was a good lunch. He saved some knowing hunger would visit again before nightfall and they would only be halfway there. The train had a dining car, but that was always expensive and a waste of money, he felt. He got up and carried his trash to the end of the car.

The car was about half full of people and, at each stop, some left and others got on. There was a mother with her young son, several service men heading home on leave, or returning to their camps. There were several men in suits and ties; probably business men heading for the big city. He was curious about a middle aged, well dressed, woman who had a look of sadness about her. On his way back to his seat, he passed her and noticed that she held a single flower with a purple ribbon around the stem. She seemed to be grieving. A war widow or mother who had lost her son? He thought of his own mother and his brother who had been killed by a deranged convict who was just let out of prison. How terrible for all of them but especially so for his mother.

After a walk to the back of the train, Bob took his seat again as the train made another of its many stops. A middle aged man got on and sat next to him after first asking if the seat was saved. Bob thought of saying that it was, but he didn't. If the fellow wanted to talk, he would talk with him. The stranger unfolded a newspaper however, and began to read.

The stranger read until he finally closed the paper, turned it to the front page again and began to read the headlines out loud. He wasn't reading to Bob particularly and Bob only half listened. Reading aloud was something people of a certain generation still did ! Whether they did it as a courtesy to those they thought couldn't read--as many older people couldn't-- or out of pride that they themselves could, he never knew. He knew that Rosie read to him because he didn't read well. His mother read to his father who didn't read at all! He glanced at the top of the paper and caught the date. It was October 1932 and no doubt beginning to get cold up north. He would do some shopping for his family for winter clothes before caming back. One headline talked about the stock market and how it was still declining. Bob's brother, Arthur, was invested in stocks. Unlike most who lost, he would make a killing and become wealthy. Bob didn't know how he did it. He had lost money in the market and wasn't anxious to ever put his own money there again.

Time, as the landscape , sped by and so did the stranger's reading. He took his paper and went into the next car. Bob opened his lunch bag again and got out the bread and cheese and thermos of water. It wasn't so cold now. He searched the bottom of the bag and below a crumpled napkin found a celery stick and carrot, and a cookie. Rosie must have added these with the orange. Again, it took the edge off his hunger.

They were coming into Richmond, Virginia. Washington would be next. Then, it would be a short hop to New York City.

Chapter 21

 $\mathcal{I}$ t was morning when the train pulled into Grand Central Station, New York. Bob went up to a counter where one could stand and eat a good breakfast at low cost. They didn't have tea and he had to order coffee. How his fellow Americans could drink this bitter stuff he could never figure out. He had grown up with an English tea drinking heritage in New England. Even loaded with sugar, he would lament that coffee tasted like crank-case oil ! The waffles and sausages he ordered were very good, however. On the way out, he bought a pack of gum and then sought a men's room. He went into his overnight bag and pulled out a clean shirt and his razor. He changed shirts, put on a bow tie, and splashed water on his face. Then, he ran a razor over his chin. Finally, he combed his hair, parting it meticulously. With grooming out of the way, he was ready to go to the street but first, he wanted to take a final look at this spectacular structure.

His eyes wandered to the very high ceiling which really needed something done to it. If he had known then what he would have to go through, some years later when called upon to paint that ceiling, he might have turned and gone back to Florida ! Briefly, it was Robert James Webb, Jr. who was responsible for painting the signs of the zodiac and mixing up all the directions of North, South, East and West on the Grand Central Station ceiling in New York City. He would tell you, however, that he was, first, not responsible for the choice of subject mater, and second, he was not responsible for the directional mix-up. He seemed to have been the only painter they could get who was insane enough to lie on his back on a scaffold, seemingly a hundred feet in the air, and paint that whole ceiling.

The reason for the mix-up was the way in which Bob had to work. Those on the ground were to hoist up the stencils, by pulley. The stencils were taped to the ceiling and paint applied. They were sent up to him in reverse and also upside down! He had no way of knowing, at such close range, that anything was wrong or what it would look like when painted until back on the ground, after the work was nearly completed. It looked spectacular and the commissioners responsible figured that no one would use it as an authentic directional guide anyway. They were more than pleased, and he was paid very well.

This work was several years in the future, however. Meanwhile, Bob was on his way from Florida to his boss's office, here in uptown New York City, to pick up instructions for his going to New Jersey and a new job; as well as collect his pay for the last church job he had done. He knew his men had already been paid but he had not. As it turned out Baum handed him a good sized check with a simple, "thank you for the church job." That chapter was closed and Bob said nothing about his men's work there. It never came up at any time in the future.

After that short cab ride to Baum's office, and a brief conversation between the two, Baum asked where he was planning to spend the night? Bob knew his architect boss would tell him of a place he could stay, or he possibly might even have a different job for him to go to. Baum was known to change his mind at the last minute. Bob was prepared. He was always ready to change his plans and go where the architect wanted to send him.

At this point, Baum had told him only about the one job in New Jersey where he and Lamb would work together. He liked the idea of working with his old teacher, Fred Lamb, and he told his employer he'd head for New Jersey right away. That's where he would spend the night. Baum said he had already talked with Lamb, who was expecting to meet Bob at his barn studio in Stoughton, Massachusetts. The paintings would be done there and transported to New Jersey.

Bob thought Lamb would probably have already gotten started on the murals and he could join him in painting and then spend the night at the home of the Lambs. It was still early in the day and that sounded good. He could have his old room back that he had when he lived with them as a boy. He liked Mrs. Lamb; she treated him as family. His work was often lonely away from his wife and children and he would like staying in their home. Mr. Lamb (as Bob always called him, out of respect) had a telephone installed in his studio. It was only beginning to be common practice to have phones in private homes. Baum called him confirming Bob's arrival. He turned the phone over to Bob, and after happy greetings,

Lamb arranged to pick up his surrogate son at the train station in Boston within a couple of hours.

Upon arrival at Lamb's studio in Stoughton, Massachusettes he could see that his old master had gotten well into the project. He had purchased very fine Irish linen-the best to paint on- and had completed the sizing and ground cover. Lamb was glad for the break in work and overjoyed to have Bobby (as he continued to call Bob) join him. The two men set work aside to get caught up on each other's lives. There was much affection between them with Lamb being more of a beloved uncle than father figure however, to Bob. Perhaps this was due to Bob's strong feeling for his natural father who was still alive. He was as close as a son to Lamb however, with the Lambs not having any children.

Lamb had made a comfortable studio out of this barn. The weather was getting colder but he had a stove and amenities for cooking. Indeed it was a studio and an apartment which was well insulated and with a full wall of glass to admit plenty of light. The two men thought it was time to get to work and Lamb loaned Bob a long painter's coat telling him to choose his weapons – paint brushes – and they would get started; there was plenty of daylight left. They worked for several hours before calling it quits and cleaning up.

Lamb then said, "Bobby, the wife has a special meal prepared for you; something I know you'll like." Bob objected that she shouldn't have done that, but in fact he couldn't wait to get "home." After two days on the train and a half day of working, he was starved. Mrs. Lamb was equally overjoyed to see her 'young man' again. Another family reunion and being shown his room, which, incidentally, looked much as it did, even to having his old fishing gear in the corner, made him truly feel at home.

They ate a typical English boiled dinner; a beef stew with dumplings that Bob was particularly fond of. They talked a long time, and went to bed early. Bob, like Lamb, was used to getting up at dawn to begin the work day. This would be a lifelong habit. Even when Bob retired and no longer had to get up early, he expected his wife and household to be up and moving about on his timetable. He was so noisy and exuberant, singing and talking to anyone or no one in particular, that one could not sleep and might as well get up!

The days would stretch out into weeks before the project was at the point where they could load it into the pickup truck and take it to the Baptist church in Montclair, New Jersey. The mural would be twenty eight feet long and seven feet high, and was painted on the best linen. The linen had been mounted on panels of manageable size to go on Lamb's truck. It would then be assembled on the walls in the church.

No day went by that Bob didn't call his wife. He was in constant touch back in Florida and grateful to his sister Jane, especially, for helping out. The phone, in Ringling's mansion, allowed for him and Rosa to talk together and share daily happenings. They also exchanged letters almost daily. Baum never complained nor did he dock Bob's pay for these calls. It was just another buisness expense.

The days and weeks he worked with Lamb were relaxing, after so much tension of new jobs and moving around; and the rather disturbing 'conversion ' of a Baptist church in Florida to Catholicism! His workers had made the mistake but he was still responsible. He had not had many failures in his vocation but this had to be a big one-- a failure of leadership he castigated himself for and he would not allow to happen again. There was also a degree of anxiety over where and when and for how long he would be working in a place. Now, the only taxing thing was arranging details for moving of his family.

About three weeks into the project, Bob decided that he should see the church. Lamb had already been there and taken measurements. It was a large Romanesque Cathedral style church with a seating capacity of nine hundred people. Both he and Lamb thought he could spend time looking for an apartment for his family while in Montclair. From there, he could go on to Florida and bring them back. He thought that within ten days or two weeks he could get these things done.

Satisfied with what he saw at the church and having met the pastor there he proceeded on his way to look for an apartment in the neighborhood. With good fortune he immediately found a second floor apartment within walking distance of the church, and a school. He called his brother in Florida, to let him know he was coming and caught the next train to New York and all points south. In a few days he picked up his truck and was back at their garage home on the Ringling estate.

Rosa was thrilled about her husband's new job, the new apartment, and the fact they would be in a town. They were not really in Sarasota, as it had not yet built up that far out. She was glad that Bob liked Harry Emerson Fosdick, the pastor of the Baptist church he would be decorating. That gave her hope that now they could go to church together as a family. Hannah, the oldest, would also be able to walk to the nearby school.

Bob had been hard to please regarding churches when Rosa had suggested they go somewhere together. He always said he was a Christian Scientist, as his mother had been, although he had never gone to that church either, after his childhood. Harry Emerson Fosdick, the pastor of the First Baptist Church, was a national figure known in about every American household by the books and inspirational pamphlets he had written. His sermons and theological writings were studied in seminaries and church schools. Bob simply liked him. He never read books and put little value in what was written in any of them except the Bible, and he wasn't always sure of that. He just took the measure of a man and could judge who he was by his bearing and speech. He trusted he would be judged the same. Besides, he had no time for reading and, if he were to admit it, he was somewhat handicaped by the limitation of his schooling.

With a storm of activity and travel-including a side trip to visit Rosa's family in North Carolina-they finally got back to their new apartment in Montclair. Bob had not forgotten their need for warm clothing and they had outfitted the children and themselves for the coming winter in the north. With his family settled into their new apartment Bob was able to get back to his job in Stoughton in just about two weeks. It wouldn't be long before he and Mr. Lamb would be through with the paintings and ready to bring them to Montclair. It would then take several years to finish the paintings and decoration of the church. He also had in mind to start looking for land in the area and begin building his and Rosa's dream home.

Chapter 22

The work on the church proceeded with the mounting of the separate painted panels onto the walls and alcoves. There was to be a painting on either side of a large stained glass Tiffany window and another at the rear of the church in a large foyer. The seams where these panels come together would have to be covered and painted. In addition, there was to be some mural painting directly on a wall. Decorative painting needed to be done throughout the church. Bob and Lamb worked together for a considerable time before Lamb went on to Boston, leaving Bob to complete the work.

Although Lamb and Bob were both aware of modern styles and techniques ushered in at the turn of the century, this particular work was of the older traditional school of realism. Bob's own style was influenced more by John Singer Sargent than by Fred Mortimer Lamb. Sargent belonged to the modern period of painting-- though some critics at the time didn't think so. He was a realist, but he saw reality with a new vision. He used strong brush strokes and vibrant primary colors loosely applied, thus giving light and air to his work.

The work in the Montclair church reflected the style of F.M. Lamb, who used somber earth colors and a controled technique in paint application. Lamb had done the preliminary drawings and some of the painting panels in his studio before Bob arrived on the scene, thus the direction of its outcome had been established. Bob did a great deal of his own painting on panels however, and took much pride in the finished project. The mural in the foyer presented a powerful narrative, seeming ready to burst from its confined space.

Lamb had left Bob with some of the direct painting on walls yet to be done. Bob related that one of the scenes he was painting had the apostles grouped around Jesus. Dr. Fosdick had confided to Bob that he was having some differences with one of the church board members. He felt he could not trust the man. Bob knew the fellow and discreetly began making sketches of him. When it came time for him to paint the portrait of Judas standing behind Jesus, Bob took out his sketches and went to work. The next day the Reverend came in early and saw what the artist had done. "Oh no! You can't do that Bob!" he exclaimed. Bob had to repaint Judas so as not to offend the church board member. He had painted a remarkable resemblance to the offending fellow.

Reverend Fosdick and members of the congregation enjoyed dropping in and watching Bob while he worked to complete the murals and do the necessary decorating. They were amazed by his skill. He would take time to tell them of work he had done for the circus man John Ringling, and how he had worked with John Singer Sargent on the Boston Public Library ceiling mural. He kept them entertained with stories of his life as a boy on the farm, a young Navy camouflage artist, or his trying to make a living as a flagpole painter, and on and on. They loved him and reached out to him and his family. His girls went to the Sunday school classes and activities the church sponsored through the week. Rosa, too, found a niche in this very warm and accepting environment.

Bob helped solve a problem in the Sunday School. Little children didn't always know where they belonged. They got lost on their way to their classroom. He took down the door to their classroom, then he had their teachers measure the children's heights. He bought lumber and framed up a new doorway and then made a new door but still looking identical to the other 'big' doors. This short one was only high enough to accommodate the tallest child of six or eight years of age! It was a charming idea, and the children were delighted. They no longer turned into the wrong room. Adults had to bend far over to come into their classroom, which amused and delighted the children and adults alike.

Montclair was one of the most affluent communities in New Jersey. Bob did decorating in the wealthy homes of parishioners and his girls had friends who lived there. As a result, he began to feel the pinch of being the next thing to poor. He couldn't keep up with his family's needs. His kids didn't dress as well, or couldn't go to some events costing money, nor could they 'keep up with the Jones'. He wasn't going to try, but was afraid his family, without being aware of it, were already trying. It caused friction in his household.

One day, he came home to find his youngest daughter sitting with a girlfriend before their refrigerator with the door open, fanning themselves. This was before the days of air conditioning and it was a very hot day. Bob asked them what they were doing and got the answer that they always did this to get cooled off! The other girl had parents who could afford to have the refrigerator running all the time, as it would with the door left open.

Bob wanted his children to have the good things of life, within reason. He provided well for his family and when they grew up and wed he outdid himself by building each of them a home for a wedding gift ! They got to choose its general location and its floor plan. It was Bob's idea that people should want and like what he gave them. The fact that they didn't always like it was disturbing to him. One daughter immediately sold the house and moved to a different part of town, though she had said this was what she had wanted.

The home he built for his young family when they first came to New Jersey in 1932 was a two-story structure on a hill at the end of a street. It was within walking distance of everything. He worked nights and weekends on it. When his parents came to New Jersey to visit, his father helped him with the construction. When he needed light to put the shingles on the roof, he parked his truck on the inclined street and turned on its lights which pointed straight at the roof and gave him just the amount of light he needed.

Of course, the neighbors were not too happy. About 1:00 a.m., some of them assembled in the yard to complain. He assured them he'd be done by dawn. Since it was a weekend, he suggested they could sleep late the next day. He put a garage on the lot, which was legal according to the zoning ordinance. At night and on weekends, he worked to convert it into a studio in which he could paint. He had in mind, also, that if he should need to rent it out in the future, it would be a nice little rental cottage. It was, for the records however, a garage. He knew what he had to do to meet his family's needs; Rosa's medical expenses alone were getting beyond what he could handle.

At one point, Rosa needed major medical attention. There was an outstanding doctor in the church from whom she was getting help. Bob also had contact with him regarding woodwork in his house. The doctor had asked him to refinish most of the elaborate woodwork in the foyer and up the winding staircase. It was a big job. Bob completed it just as Rosa's therapy was completed. As Bob was picking up his last drop-cloths and tools, the doctor came home and asked him how much it was going to cost. Bob, in turn, asked him how much his wife's therapy would cost. The doctor, at that point suggested that they consider their bills paid as one professional to another. They confirmed this transaction with an amiable handshake.

On another occasion, Bob had a wealthy client who didn't want to pay his bill. The work had been completed and the bill presented. It was well within the estimated amount and the client said he was satisfied with the work. Several weeks went by, and then a month, but still he did not pay. Reminders went out once, twice, and that was enough. The man was at his work place each day. His servants were seen coming and going. He had a big party, which said that he was obviously enjoying the luxurious new look Bob had given his home.

Bob wasn't about to put up with such nonsense. One day, he stationed himself across the street from the man's house. After the man left for work, Bob went to the door and rang the bell. The butler answered. Bob stepped in and proceeded to taking down the very thick, elaborately carved front door, which had been imported from Italy. He took the door out to his truck and threw it in. He told the butler to tell his boss he would get his door back when he paid what he owed him. The client paid that same day.

Chapter 23

Reverend Harry Emerson Fosdick and his pastoral associates showed an interest in Bob Webb. They knew that he was articulate and his life experiences made him interesting. They drew him into their circle and invited him to both their social and intellectual activities. He had never encountered anything like this before. They spent hours in theological debate and after presenting the various sides of an argument would ask Bob what he thought. Bob never hesitated to tell them what he thought. He knew he was out of his element, but he never felt inferior to anyone. His logic and storehouse of experiences lent credence to what he said, and he felt that they could accept it or not as they pleased.

Bob came to the conclusion that with all their

questioning and debate, some were thinking themselves out of their own belief! One fellow became so disturbed in his effort to understand and his judgment of himself was so harsh, he committed suicide. It happened right at their meeting, in the presence of everyone!

There was a doctor with their group and, for some reason, the discussion had turned to methods of killing oneself. This unstable individual asked the doctor to show him exactly how it could be done with a knife; how to hold it and where to insert it, and at what angle. Having shown the victim, the doctor turned away from the fellow, who then pulled out a knife and did just as he had been shown! Bob and the others present were horrified. Nothing could be done for the man before he was gone; it happened so quickly and successfully as the doctor had demonstrated. The fellow had been at the head of the table and he slumped over into his own pool of blood forming beneath him and beginning to run down the table and spread out in five directions from the ends of his fingers toward each of the men present. Bob jumped up and all he could see was a flashback memory from his childhood of five fingers and their stumps from which blood was pumping out.

It had been a recall from the time he was five

years old and had accidentally chopped off the fingers of the right hand of his best friend! His father had given him an ax and told him to go catch a chicken and kill it for their dinner. After catching the bird he had asked his friend to hold it down for him. Bob's mother and the boy's mother had also been the best of friends. This moment of tragedy had altered their lives. This moment here today would be catastrophic for many.

Though Bob's mother said her son's action was an accident, Bobby felt it was his fault and his guilt could not be relieved. Bob, now the man, was angry with this church fellow for imposing his tragedy on them. He put his hands to his face and groaned. Turning away from the scene, he left the church and once outside bent over and lost his lunch. Going straight home he told his wife what had happened and went to his garage studio.

He had a little wood stove in his studio and started a fire. He felt cold. With much effort he prepared a canvas and began to paint. Later when finished, he sat and studied his work for a long time. It was a painting unlike any he had ever done or would ever do again. He then cut it from it's stretcher-frame and opening the door to the rooring fire he stuffed the painting in. That was the end of it. It had expressed a tragedy he could now forget; it would always have a place in his memory but as a reference and not as a prominent thought. Life was important; he had responsibilities and had to live free of such distraction. He prayed it be gone from him. Crossing the street, he went back to work on a porch he was repairing for his neighbor.

The times were very hard in the 1930's during the depths of the great depression. People were not able to cope and had begun to act in all kinds of deviant ways because they didn't know what to do. The whole country seemed to be falling apart. Bob thought they waited too long to take any positive action about their situations and were frozen with fear until, like some brittle thing, they broke. Each had his private tragedy. Bob had come to know these church people and their problems were not so different than his own. He concluded that everyone had serious problems and that work, any kind of work, would help. A person could not remain inactive-frozen-without consequences.

It was time for him to leave here. Years had gone by and his work had been finished in the church. Lamb had left and come back only once to see it completed. There was nothing more for him to do in the church. Even though these people had invited him to their study group and wanted him to stay, he had nothing more to give or gain by staying. The pastor and his parishioners had problems. According to Bob's account, tragic events followed and compounded within that church. He had no part in it. His life was elsewhere. He looked forward to more creative work when architects would begin to build again.

Bob was making his living by painting and decorating in homes of the wealthy who could still afford such work, in Montclair. He had built his home here but would move and build again for a permanent job of his liking.

Things started to change at the end of the thirties, as the depression released it's grip on the nation. Bob picked up the commission of painting the Grand Central Station ceiling, he decorated a big Y.M.C.A. in New York City, did a hotel lobby mural, and also decorated a large estate on the Hudson River. He frequently went to New York City to various architect's offices where such work was assigned, although it was D.J.Baum who gave him most of the work he had through those trying years.

His wife had been diagnosed with Parkinson's Disease, and continued to require a full time personal maid. Bob very much wanted a steady job in one place where he could come home each night and take care of her until he retired. He had always wanted to put down roots, have a permanent home, and friends of his own kind he could share good and bad times with. He wanted at least what his parents had enjoyed, stability and a home. He knew he should not complain when many where going without food and a place to live in the depression of the 1930's.

Chapter 24

Bob Webb seemed to live by a faith that worked for him. He never talked about religion but he did have beliefs which were rooted in his childhood experiences, perhaps by going to church with his mother who had such a direct influence on him. He never doubted his commitment to the field of art and, like most artists, he saw his motivation to paint as something coming from outside of himself, something given to him; what many refer to as a 'calling.' He never questioned it or doubted he could make a living doing what he had chosen as his lifes work.

He knew that the kind of work he had experience in was out there and it would continue to come his way through the New York architects. He only had to say "yes" when it did come. Meanwhile he would continue to do easel paintings to satisfy his urge to paint. He would make sure of an income he needed by continuing to paint houses. There was work enough to 'keep the wolf away' and satisfy the needs of his family. The occasional creative projects were as icing on the cake.

An overview of the life of Bob Webb shows there were some fallow times but these where balanced by amazing flashes of good fortune and opportunities that he took advantage of. Thus it was that one day his old boss D.J.Baum called him to come into his office. There Bob met his future employer and the job he would have for the rest of his working days. It was not only the kind of work he was experienced in but it would answer the need he had for friends of his own choosing. He had been missing people of his own age and the comradely of his youth; men who could hunt and fish and party together. These would be people hired by his new employer, the Colonial Williamsburg Foundation.

Many individuals have heard varied accounts from Bob of how it was that he got employed by the Colonial Williamsburg Foundation. Bob never seemed to tell a story the same way twice! His stories were true but varied in that some were more inclusive than others. Some had a dramatic emphasis, or differed as to time or location. He would limit or condense or combine elements of an event to make it better for the telling. He told of having an appointment with D.J.Baum when the architect walked out of his office with a man he introduced as John D. Rockefeller Jr. Rockefeller struck up a conversation that revealed he knew Bob had worked for the National Lead Company and that he had decorated the Ringling Mansion. He told Bob he needed an artist down in Williamsburg, Virginia and went on to discribe the position. When finished he asked Bob if he would be interested. It would be a permanent position.

How, Mr Rockefeller described his adventure of a big investment in Wlliamsburg isn't known. Whether Bob offered his own experience of spending two hours in that village when he was a naval recruit is not known. Bob said their conversation was mostly about him and his background. Bob did say he knew that Mr. Rockefeller had taken on quite a challenge in the restoration of the town. He quoted Mr. Rockefeller as saying he needed people who would make it authentic as to what it was back in the 1770's. Bob was hired to take part in that dramatic transformation.

It would go from the decay and neglect of his day to what it had been two hundred years ago in the 1770s. Then a governor, appointed by the king of England, lived in Williamsburg and ruled over the colony of Virginia. The Govenor's Palace would need restoring and repainting inside and out. The palace was only one structure needing restoration. The whole town would be rebuilt and brought to life with costumed people living there as they did in the 18th century! It would be a living museum and history lesson for those who would come and visit it.

Tourists would not only see how people lived and worked then but, with actors performing, could observe some of the events that shaped our history. Thomas Jefferson, Patrick Henry and George Washington met there and helped to unify the colonies and egnite a revolution. The painter from Massachusettes, Robert Webb, was awed by having a part in so important a project as to rebuild this historic town. It brought out the patriot in him that was so deeply a part of his character.

Not only would Bob initially identify and make the colors of the original 18th Century buildings, but he would be heading up the painting and decorating department with a crew of men under him. Mr. Rockefeller told Bob that he would have to first be approved by Mr. Chorley, C.E.O. of the Foundation, before being hired officially. Bob was given a telephone number to call for an appointment. He made the call immediately, got the interview, and was hired.

Those hired by the Foundation were required to undergo a six month, on the job, trial period before becoming permanent. Bob had no trouble with this, and proved to be a good and loyal worker. When his trial period was up, he wrote a letter to Mr. Chorley thanking him for giving him this opportunity to work for the Colonial Williamsburg Foundation. He defined what he was doing on the job, and told how he was caring for the tools, the shop, and the men he was responsible for. He made a copy of his letter to keep. It was well written and reads as a very gracious letter of thanks.

Bob felt as if he had spent his whole life in preparation for this job. He had always led men in their work, from his Navy days to the Ringling mansion, to church decorating. Mr. Rockefeller said he wanted a color artist; Robert Webb had a reputation as the best colorist in the field. He could work with architects and give them what they wanted in decorating. He was dependable, sober- on the job at least, and always willing to work flexible hours and take on a variety of jobs as needed.

The year was 1940, and the nation was once again at war. He recalled, some twenty plus years earlier, as a young Navy recuit, being let off a train with a flat wheel and told to explore this town of Williamsburg, Virginia for a couple of hours. Looking at it now, it had changed very little. It still had a long way to go before taking on the clean look of the 1770s capital and political hotbed of the nation. What he particularly remembered seeing were the cows and horses, sheep and goats grazing on the village green, probably as they did in the 1700's. He looked around and wondered where he was supposed to live until he could settle his family in this new environment.

When he asked where he could stay while on the job and not yet having a permanent home, someone, unbelievably, suggested there was a garage around the corner! He went out looking for it and found it, as he had been told, just around the corner off the village green. It had no door and only a shower with a pull chain to drop the cold water, a wash basin, and a toilet. The shower was directly across from a doorless opening ; at night, he found that people were parking their cars and watching him take his shower! Ringling's garage was a mansion by comparison. At least, he didn't have to bring his family here! He would go out looking for something better but would have to stay here till he found it. The many 'Bread and Breakfast' establishments that would proliferate in coming years were not even a thought then.

Chapter 25

$\mathcal{B}$ob had started his job and was looking over the color samples neatly arranged on a peg board hanging beside his desk. The National Lead Company had also recommended him for this position, and he knew they were responsible for making this chart with individual little chips of each color. They had used all the primary colors first used by the early settlers. Here were the 17 secondary colors also painted on chips, and the 60 colors that could be made from the different combinations of the 17. These were the total of what the villagers had to choose from in whatever painting they had to do inside and out. Sixty was the full range of their colors and nothing more. Over time, Bob and Dean Moorehead, from the architecture department, would work to make exact formulas for these. They actually mixed up large quantities for storage and future use on the buildings and in the interiors Bob and his men would be responsible for maintaining.

As the superintendant of the paint shop, Robert Webb, together with architects, and a research chemist determined the color of each house and building on the grounds. They did this by stripping the original 18th Century doors of their paints layer by layer to determine the various colors of each new paint job done by the colonists. The last-original- color was then used for that house and given the name of the structure it represented, such as Wythe House Gold which was a yellow ochre color.

The architects and archaeologist researched each house and building and determined its exact size, location, color, and everything about it. They worked from papers on record in Williamsburg and also in England. Old engravings and photos confirmed the looks of a structure. Some that were still standing had changed very little down through the years. Some had additions that required removing. In time Rockefeller had acquired all the houses and public buildings in the old city and was in process of restoring them to their 18th century look. It would take decades to complete.

In the establishment of Colonial Wlliamsburg the Foundation had only a few problems with the community, in the beginning. One in particular, that Bob remembered, had to do with a house bought from a citizen who felt that it was worth a lot more money than what he got for it from Mr. Rockefeller. The house needed renovation with new dormers put on the two sides of the slanted roof. Not being able to locate an old engraving, the architects didn't know whether there had been three or four dormers on each side. They took a chance and put only three on. The citizen-former owner- watched them every day until they were finished. He then walked up and presented them with a two hundred year old engraving he had been keeping. It showed not three but four dormers !

Purists that they were, the architects took the roof off and started over, reconfiguring it for the four dormers. The disgruntled former owner went away feeling satisfied that he had gotten even for not getting the price he thought he had deserved for his house. People felt very pressured to sell and the prices did get better as the citizenry began to find out who was actually buying their properties. Those who sold early, at a lower price, were naturally disgruntled later on.

Mr.Rockefeller was able to keep his name

out of the dealings for a long time. Thus there was not always a happy coexistence between the town's people and the historic village. In time however, the citizens of the "new" Williamsburg that had grown up around the old village, and those displaced by Mr. Rockefeller, were happy, as they prospered from the Colonial Capital's tourism and influx of commerce and cultural events.

Bob took advantage of the flexibility offered him to do what was necessary to get settled. He decided to take time and go into the new Williamsburg and find a decent place to live. Rosa and their youngest daughter, Thelma, were still in New Jersey, and would stay there until he found a place for them. Their oldest daughter, Hannah, had entered nurses training and he thought she would join them later. It happened however, that she got married and started her own life. Her husband was in the military and Bob wouldn't see much of them for awhile. Continuing to look for a place to live, he didn't have to go far from his job site to find a rental on Capital Landing Road. It was big enough to meet their needs and close enough to his shop that he could ride a bicycle to work.

The management of the historic area, which was known as Colonial Williamsburg or just

C.W., already had rules and procedures. One, almost from the beginning, was that there would be no motor vehicles allowed in the historic area. Workers would have to walk or ride a horse or conveyance consistent with 18th Century transportation. This would have to be modified somewhat later on, for expediency. Bob's workplace, assigned to him by Mr. Chorley, although in the historic area, was at the outermost perimeter. He asked if he could ride a bicycle and was given permission. After scouting the few business places in the new Williamsburg without any luck in finding a bike, he headed for Newport News, which was a larger, more commercially developed area.

This was again familiar ground going back to his Navy days twenty years earlier. Again it was busy with activity, as World War 11 was in full swing. The nostalgia of this Chesapeake Bay experience was overwhelming to him. This is where he became a man with responsibilities beyond his own immediate needs. He met his wife here. He boarded submarines in war time and looked through their periscopes to get a view of how the Germans would see our ships in the bay or out at sea. He was sent up in a Navy balloon to get a wider scope of the Bay. He was shackled to a prisoner and took him to Boston on a train to stand trial for murder. He pursued a German submarine crew through the James River swamps. The camouflage work he did here was unique and copied throughout the Navy.

After his death he was recognized by a medal and a certificate of appreciation from the President of the United States, Ronald Reagan, for his "devoted and selfless consecration to his country..." All of these events (deserving of the recognition he received posthumously) were alive in his memory as he scouted the area. One could see how his attention could be drawn away from the immediate purpose of finding a bicycle.

Everything had changed and he was a bit disoriented. He decided to come back some day soon and visit his old haunts again. Today, he had come on a shopping tour. He had driven his truck and parked it on an incline with a view of the bay and the fleet. The ships looked huge as they lay side by side high in the water. A tugboat with a man on the deck looked like a speck beside them. It would be a job to paint one of those today, he reflected, as he put his old truck in gear and went looking for a cycle shop.

It had been a long time since he had ridden a bike, but he knew he could, and would have no trouble. He found one and, for his daughter's amusement, named it 'The Blue Goose ' after his sister's boyfriend's racing skiff. He had sailed on it once when his sister made good with her promise to arrange a trip for him in exchange for his painting shown at the Boston Museum of Art, when he was a boy of twelve. He would not go so fast as they had on the Blue Goose, though he would speed up to show his daughter, Thelma, he could still ride a bike.

There was no traffic in the little cow town of Williamsburg, Virginia, and he had to be more careful of sheep, ducks and cows crossing his path than people. "Heavy traffic" consisted of a cart pulled by oxen and a buckboard pulled by mules.

Chapter 26

One day, Bob was surprised by what he saw as he entered the yard of his paint shop. He couldn't believe such a fancy carriage as this, parked in the lot before him, still existed. He hadn't seen one since he was an apprentice with Mr. Lamb and Lamb had "loaned him" to help an old man restore a carriage with a family crest on it. The old artist worked exclusively for museums lucky enough to find such heirloom carriages. To restore them required special paints and a special skill calling for a knowledge of heraldry. There is a school of heraldry in Scotland where this old painter had studied. Bob felt fortunate to have had this experience of working with him and learning from his unique skills.

In England and in America at the time of

the colonies, wealthy families and royalty had their own family crests which were painted on carriages and sometimes hung as banners in churches. The old man had taught Bob what he knew and assigned him to do the striping, which was a challenge. It took a steady hand to paint a narrow straight line, or stripe, all the way around the carriage and meet up with it where he had started. Bob knew what striping was, as in the early days of automobiles, striping on them was an added luxury. He had heard that women were usually hired to do this. Whether they had a steadier hand or not he didn't know.

How to restore the crests was a lost art, even when Bob was a boy. He felt lucky to be able to draw on this early apprentice experience to restore the carriages at Colonial Williamsburg. He knew he would have to make the paints himself.

The C.W. Foundation had three family carriages that would require regular maintenance. The carriage he found parked at his shop was driven by a retired cavalry man, Colonel Downing, who had been hired as the horseman who always drove the carriages. He sat straight in his magisterial uniform and, with gloved hands, held the reins of a very handsome stallion. Downing exuded importance as he related to Bob his position of responsibility for all the horses at Colonial Williamsburg. Bob walked around examining the crest and could see that the paint was beginning to alligator, that is wrinkle up. This process is due to age and exposure to weather. In time, it would flake off. He relayed to Dowing what had to be done.

Colonel Downing wanted to stay and watch what Bob would do to repair the crest. Of course, Bob guarded what he knew and would not permit this. He would never give an answer to inquiries of how he did something unless it was already widely known by everyone but the inquirer. He said he had worked too long and too hard without any pay to give away what he now knew. In doing this, he was following a guild tradition hundreds of years old. It made sense then because nobody wanted another to copy their knowledge and take away their livelihood. Not that the carriage driver could do that, as Bob soon found out. He realized that Colonel Downing had tried to correct the alligatoring of the paint himself and had damaged the crest even further. Now, it would take more work to bring it back. Bob delighted in the challenge.

On Monday after their evening meal he and Rosa got in the truck and drove over to the paint shop. Since in years past they could never be together while Bob worked, this was a great pleasure to them. They parked just off the historic grounds and went to where the Colonel had parked the carriage to be painted. It was no longer there; Bob had asked his men to mop the floor inside the shop and partition off a work area just for the carriage. They had already washed it and pulled it inside through the shop's double garage doors. All of this was to make sure no dust would settle on the new paint when completed.

He pulled up a chair for Rosa who had brought a book to read, and adjusted the spotlights on his own work. This would be the coat of arms for the Randolph Payton carriage. It had alligatored and it appeared that Downing had tried to remove the roughness with something abrasive. Bob opened the carriage door and with tools and some steady work, removed the hinge bolts and took the door to a table and laid it flat. He then proceeded to apply a solvent to relax the old pigment.

Proceeding step by step, after cleaning up the damage that had been done, he put the door back on. The actual painting of the crest could now begin. Time went by and he was completely lost in his work. Rosa was lost in her book. Suddenly, Bob looked up and said, "Where's Thelma?" Their youngest said she would be home late after attending a meeting at a friend's house.

Bob was glad she had come to Williamsburg

with them though she had first wanted to stay in New Jersey with friends. Still a teenager, she gave up a job and a boyfriend to help her parents move. She had already dropped out of school but could have continued in Williamsburg if she had wanted to. Her father did not press her to go on to high school telling her she could do as well as he had without an education. Both parents wanted her with them. She was lively and brought fun and youth and, it might be added, help in the home to her parents.

"Speak of the devil!" Bob exclaimed, laughing, as he looked to the door and Thelma walked in. He couldn't help himself as he asked, "Where have you been?" Long after she was married and had children, he knew he would be looking out for her and wondering where she was.

Their oldest daughter, Hannah, being married was no longer a worry to them. Thelma would need her father and he was always there to support her. He was her strength through the death of her first husband and the tragic loss of a child, and the lose of her mother, as well as through her four more marriages, and his own remarriage to a younger woman whom she was never able to accept. He knew he wouldn't get any more work done in the paint shop. They all might as well pile into the truck and go home, which they did.

Back at work the next day, Bob began to organize the paint shop. The carriage was a special job that could wait for evenings and weekends. He made plans for the various duties his new crew would perform. In hiring painters, he was as limited as the other new department heads. They all had to choose from the people who came to apply for their unique type of job. None of them were painters. They were fishermen, farmers, tradesmen. Many owned the land and buildings John D.RockefellerJr. bought up, and were displaced not only from their homes but many from their security and life work. They were paid well for their properties, but were very aggressively encouraged to sell. They simply didn't have the time or hadn't thought ahead as to where they would go or what they would do afterwards.

Others, such as women and young people just out of school, were seeking work for the first time. They became the costumed people who posed as shop owners or tour guides in the historic village. Most had to be taught their jobs. These would be as varied as that of printer, wig maker, basket weaver, cooper or barrel maker, baker, candlestick makers. They were called reenactors. Later on, employees would become people from across the nation, drawn to Colonial Williamsburg out of a love for their country, or desire to be a part of this living history experiment.

The workers who were doing the day to day labor of putting the historic town together dressed normally as 20th Century people. Those posing as 18th Century historical workers or residents dressed in 18th Century costume. Bob required his men to wear modern white painter's pants and shirt. He held an inspection of them every morning; much as if they were in the Navy! As Superintendant of the Paint Shop he wore a 20th century suit, white shirt usually, and tie.

A cannon went off late in the day every day at the same time over by the magazine, the place where munitions were kept. Fife and drummers in uniform paraded. They were mostly Williamsburg high school students doing after school work for a little pay. Bob headed out across the campus to look in on his men at work. Whether painting weatherboards on a house with white lead or tarring and sanding wooden shingles, they were ready to quit when they saw him coming late in the afternoon. They began to fold things up and call it a day.

Chapter 27

Saturdays and Sundays were not exempt from the work ethic of Robert Webb. He could be found in the paint shop repairing a wooden Indian or other artifact from the Abby Aldrich Folk Art Museum. Mary Black, Director of the Museum, sent much work to him for restoration. He had other things he wanted to do on these days, as well. He would visit his friends who were the cook and chauffeur of the Rockefellers. He was welcome in their kitchen at Bassett Hall, where the stock pot was always on the stove with a meat and vegetable broth simmering. After a brief visit and bowl of soup, Bob continued his walk to the end of the Duke of Glouster Street where old Judge Armstead lived.

Judge Armstead was the last holdout; he

wouldn't sell his home to the Foundation. He vowed he never would sell. It was considered by C.W. personel to be an eyesore that stood out, being the only 19th Century Victorian mansion in a village of simple 18th Century colonial residences. Bob liked "the stubborn old goat," as he called him, and frequently stopped by his house to pass the time of day. Sometimes, the two men would go fishing together. Judge Armstead liked to catch carp and take them to some citizens he frequently saw on the other side of the bench. He said they knew how to prepare carp in a special way so as to be edible.

After watching the sun become a big red feather, painting the whole of the historic village in a wash of red-orange, with the day nearly gone, Bob would go home and spend the evening with Rosie as he always called her. She was still able to read the paper to him though she had difficulty holding it steady.

One day, early in his employment, while returning to the paint shop, Bob was crossing the village green and sensed someone catching up with him. He looked to his left and saw Mr. Rockefeller stride for stride beside him. He spoke first, asking Bob how he liked his work. He asked next how Bob's wife was doing. Then, he gestured to a bench and asked Bob to sit down with him. Bob took a seat and waited patiently, trying to get a feel for the man. Something was on his mind, and Bob knew that he would finally tell him.

"Webb, this is a Southern town, and I have a real problem here. I notice you have a couple of Negroes on your staff. How has that worked out with the other men? What do they think about it?" Bob answered, "Mr. Rockefeller, I don't care what they think. I hire people for the job they can do. If someone doesn't like it, let them leave." Rockefeller went on to tell him there were signs (which had been there before Bob's time) saying, 'whites only' on drinking fountains, restrooms and benches that would be offensive to a lot of visitors to the historic area. "There will be tourists coming from other countries where the people are dark. How do we handle this?" Rockefeller inquired.

Bob said, "That's easy. Just tell me to send my men out to pick up all those signs and bring in all the benches for repainting. I'll have them all sanded and repainted without the 'whites only.' They'll be in and out so fast no one will even know they were gone." Rockefeller tersely responded, "Do It ! Thank you Webb, I knew you could get it done," and he got up and left. That afternoon, Bob had all the offending signs and benches rounded up and in the shop. Men were assigned to stripping them of their offensive words and repainting them a solid color. By the next afternoon they were back where they came from.

After that, over the years, Bob would sometimes be in his office at his desk and look up to see Mr. Rockefeller walk in. He might sit down to pass the time of day, or ask Bob to take a walk. Usually, this was preliminary to asking Bob if he could get away for a couple of days. He would want him to do a decorating job for a friend's estate or some other project in New York. They would meet at the little airport in Williamsburg and fly together in Rockefeller's plane to some estate or some landing strip near where he would be working.

Bob never let anyone know about this. He wanted to be on a level with his co-workers and not have them think he was getting special treatment. They did wonder and thought he was just taking off and going home early. Everyone knew his wife was very ill and sometimes he was needed at home even though he had a full time maid for her. He would never leave her alone overnight and would have someone stay with her after his daughter left home.

Secrets are hard to keep however, and when a

second paycheck would come into the office from New York, someone would tell someone and the 'cat was out of the bag'. His buddies began to inquire, "Where did you go this time, Webb?" He didn't want to make an adventure out of it nor appear favored by the boss, Mr Rockefeller.

The best course was simply to say he had other work to do elswhere.

One place he could drive to, and also take some friends with him, was the estate of the daughter of Walter Chrysler, the auto giant. He did a lot of decorative work in their home. She had married a popular sports figure 'for love'. His name was Garbisch. They had a large estate in Maryland with many caretaker houses and even their own church and parsonage on the grounds. Bob was very well liked there, and they invited him back over and over again through the years. He took a good friend of his, Floyd, who also worked at C.W., with him a couple of times.

After many years and after Bob had finished building his home on Neck-O-Land Road, his old truck had about seen its last days. On one of his trips to Maryland, the Garbisch couple noticed Bobs old truck and the trouble he was having starting it. They knew his pay was minimal at Colonial Williamsburg and knew he had a philosophy of paying cash for whatever he purchased. He was certainly in the need of a new car. He no longer needed a truck, having finished all the building he intended to do at his home site. Being rather tall, he needed a car with head room. Without telling him, they were taking the measure of the man!

They learned that his birthday was but a few weeks away which gave them time to put an order in for a new Chrysler New Yorker, four door, fully automated seats, windows, doors, and with air-conditioning ! A dark green sedan was ordered to be delivered on his birthday with a big red ribbon spread over the top. Needless to say, Bob was overwhelmed when he looked out the kitchen window early that morning and saw it parked there. How could he thank them? They made it easy for him assuring him of their friendship and devotion to him and his wife. He said it was too fancy a car for a simple country fellow but he needed a car and was grateful to them. He and Rosie would enjoy it. He took good care of it, washing the motor with a toothbrush annually! In the intervening years he put over two hundred thousand miles on the guage, going mostly to Florida.

The day that her husband died, Bernice Garbisch called Bob at his home in Williamsburg and said she wanted to say goodbye to him. She explained that she and her husband had a pact that whoever died first, the other would follow immediately. They were elderly and neither wanted the other to have to go through what settlement of so vast an estate would entail. They feared all the 'vultures' she said, who would inevitably come down upon them.

Bob talked with her for some time, making a futile effort to dissuade her from what she was about to do. He cried that evening, knowing he had failed and had lost a good friend. About a week later, a notice of a double funeral appeared in the newspaper. Another friend gone and, with his own impending retirement he knew he should feel older but he didn't. He could never think of taking his own life. This was wrong, regardless of circumstances.

Chapter 28

In time, John D. Rockefeller 111, took over the management of The Colonial Williamsburg Foundation from his father. After him, there were others. They all made changes until a major reconstruction occured. Many 'old -timers' didn't like the new structure, feeling that the educational purpose was being sacrificed simply for the making of money. Bob withheld judgement, looking forward to retirement, he rode the waves of change.

In the intervening years since Bob's retirement, management turned things around and the 'Old Timers' would be happy with things as they developed through time. Colonial Williamsburg has been recognized for serving its purpose as a living museum and educational institution of the highest caliber. Bob would say that in his day it also lived up to its goals. His grandchildren and great grandchildren, as grade school youngsters, spent summers with him and enjoyed their learning experiences at Colonial Williamsburg as have people of all ages.

Before Mr. Rockefeller Jr. retired, he made one more major purchase of a building and land. It was a necessary acquisition to the historic city and proved to be of great benefit to the City of Williamsburg and to the Commonwealth of Virginia. A hard fought compromise gave the Foundation the grounds and building of the historic psychiatric hospital known in the eighteenth century as 'The Lunatic Asylum.' It sat squarely in a strategic part of Colonial Williamsburg and there was nothing to be done but to recognize it and incorporate it into the plans for the village.

A decision was made to maintain it as a museum showing the gruesome treatment of the mentally ill in 18th Century America. Many of the original devices of chains and leg irons, straight- jackets, primitive syringes and saws for performing surgeries on the brain were all still there. Devices for punishment also showed the thinking of our 18th century ancestors as believing mental illness to be a faked choice of the inmate, therefore deserving punishment. Some syringes, from a later period, possibly to ease pain or quiet agitation, were also displayed.

Later, this museum was relegated to a small area in a remote part of the building. The larger portion then became a museum of artifacts from archaeological finds and donations of period furniture. It was made more comfortable for the modern tourist by fresh coats of paint in a warmer, brighter hue. Mr. Rockefeller gave many millions of dollars to buy land and build a new state of the art psychiatric facility in the new Williamsburg outside the Colonial Capital.

The new modern hospital could rival any medical facility in the country. It enjoyed a medical-surgical unit and facilities for including art therapy, music, physical education, occupational and other therapies. The campus had a swimming pool and tennis courts. This was a very costly exchange for the Colonial Williamsburg Foundation and it can be said that the Commonwealth of Virginia was the better off.

After Bob's work crew had completed the painting of the new museum he took a walk to check it out and continued on to the shops and work areas of the historic village. As he walked around, stopping at various places where his men were working, he knew the individuals who assumed the roles of barrel maker – called the cooper – the wig maker, type-setter in the print shop, music master, who taught the young ladies how to play the harpsichord, the bookmaker, the candle and soap makers, and many others. Of course, what interested him especially was the bread-baker who turned out loaves from great stone and brick fireplaces designed with cubical openings to keep the bread warm for rising, as well as baking. He continued on to the Williamsburg Inn.

There he met a young man who played a violin in the dinning room while strolling among the tables. Outside again, he proceeded on to where the blacksmith, working at his anvil, sent sparks from molton hot metal as he pounded it into tools and utensils. There where sheep and horses and mules and oxen in stalls, with a crew of workers tending them. Many of these exhibits reminded Bob of his own youth before the days of the motor car, supermarkets, and mass production of everything.

Chapter 29

*B*ob had men from his paint shop working in all of the exhibition areas as they needed upkeep. He liked the diversity here which ment that each new project was a challenge. He liked working with the architects and sharing the technical details for making paint formulas and finishes. They researched and shared with him historic patterns for specific signs, murals, and decorative motifs that he would employ in various places throughout the village. He would bring his technical skills to bear in executing each of these new projects.

He noted the lack of signs telling tourists what the various shops were that they saw on their walk through the historic village. The architecture department was in process of remedying that, and

Bob would soon have a part to play in making the signs. Most people who lived in the 18th Century couldn't read, so the signs were a picture language telling people what to expect inside each shop. A simple boot, a hat, a wig, a stein of beer, a loaf of bread and a steaming cup, all invited the shopper to enter as his need directed.

The architecture department sent people to England to track down what signs actually looked like in the colonies. The tavern signs, apothecary, bookmaker and all the rest were found in old lithographs or as illustrations in period publication in the England of the 1770s. These were mostly in archives of libraries or in museums. Pictures were taken and copies made of these and brought back to the paint shop. Bob made drawings from them and cut stencils for painting the signs on wood. Metal hooks were inserted, and they were hung on posts at the appropriate sites around the village. Having in mind that one day they would need repainting, Bob kept the stencils on file. The large coat of arms, placed on the Capital Building, was painted freehand, however. With pride Bob told how he had painted this placard and that it had lasted there for eighteen years before needing restoration.

The projects and the diversity of work he

had to do at Colonial Williamsburg, gave Bob the incentive to want an apprentice. As he had learned from a master so he wanted to teach a young person skills to be passed on to a new generation. From master to apprentice was the old way he was familier with. He asked those who employed workers to send him a young person who exhibited an interest in art and had talent.

He said that he never found a young person who was willing to spend the time to learn decorating or painting conservation. Whether they had a background or not they only wanted to be paid well for a limited and circumscribed range of work assigned to them. On the other hand, he reflected, they were willing to pay to go to an art school! He complained that no one he ever hired sustained an interest in his line of specialties for a long enough time to really learn. Conservation particularly was something that took time and infinate patience.

The historic village needed these services and Bob had one or two workers experienced enough to carry out more creative work. The folk art museum needed a painting conservator and Bob was the only one able to do this work. He loved doing it but he wanted to train another. Also a variety of decorative work was required in the exhibition areas, the motels, and display areas with artifacts. He had a good sign painter on his staff and good exterior and interior painters. There was no shortage of talent in the paint shop. However, one more with artistic skills would have been welcomed.

Much later, away from Colonial Williamsburg, well after retirement, and now a widower, Bob did find an already accomplished artist who was interested in painting restoration. He didn't want to lose her so he married her! But that is a later story.

Bob could claim the title of 'Master'. He and his wife Rosa were invited to Richmand, Virginia to the annual meeting of the Virginia Chapter of the American Institute of Architects. There Robert Webb, Jr. was presented with a Certificate of Award for, " High standards and recognized skill as a MASTER CRAFTSMAN in the field of Architectural Painting and especially for the wide variety of decorative and pictorial painting he has executed for the Restoration of Colonial Williamsburg."

In accepting this award Bob turned to his wife in the audience and said, "Whatever I am and whatever I've been able to do I owe to my wife, Rosa," and he blew her a kiss. This was received with applause.

Bob gave little thought to the difficult route

of practical experience it took for him to excel in his work. Any beginner, in one way or another, would have had to travel a similar route. An art school education would be an equivalant today. Bob saw such schooling as a step in the right direction and he might have taught in such a setting himself! He was invited to do so at the College of William and Mary in Williamsburg, but declined.

Chapter 30

One of the highlights of Bob's years in Colonial Williamsburg was the visit of Queen Elizabeth and Prince Phillip. When he learned that Queen Elizabeth and Prince Phillip of England would be visiting the Colonial Capital, Bob was excited. He had a special affinity for England, his parents having come from there. The Queen and her consort would be arriving on rather short notice, thus putting the foundation into a frenzy of preparation.

The Royal couple would spend the night at the Williamsburg Inn. This was the historic capital's finest hotel and had always held a five star rating. Management did feel, however, that the suite for the royals needed a coat of paint, and called Bob and his crew of painters in to get the job done. The Foundation's rule to strictly adhere to the use of authentic paints presented a problem that modern water based paints would not have. Not only were they slower in drying, but they had a strong odor that took days to be rid of. Bob's men proceeded and got the painting done with two days to spare. The management came in to examine the work and were alarmed by the smell. Bob told them not to worry; he would take care of it.

He went to the Inn's kitchen and asked to borrow all the cookie sheets, large pans, and whatever other containers they could spare. He then sent two men out to the local markets to buy up all the apples they could get. They returned with something like three bushel baskets full. He then set his crew to work cutting the apples into pieces and distributing them around the rooms, under the beds, and wherever an empty space was found. He told everyone to come back in the morning and they would be surprised and satisfied.

Some heads wagged and grumbling could be heard, but they had to give Webb a chance. What else could they do at this late date? It would be hard to find a more royal setting for the Queen in all of Williamsburg. They would wait and see. When morning came, they entered the Queen's chambers with trepidation and were pleasantly surprised. They were more than surprised. They were satisfied and delighted! The apples had absorbed the odor and left the rooms with a sweet springtime freshness everyone was happy with. The Royal Couple could now arrive anytime.

One of the events planned for Queen Elizabeth and Prince Phillip was to attend Sunday services at the historic Bruton Parish Church. A congregation of select townspeople were invited to this first Church of England in America, now an Episcopal church. The Reverend W.A.R. Goodwin delivered a stirring sermon. It was his influence and early research that had interested Mr. Rockefeller in financing and reconstructing the 18th Century historic Williamsburg! Goodwin continued to be a voice in the community for the many years he was Rector of the parish.

A small church, it was interesting for its original appointment of waist-high pew enclosures with an entry door, a bench and a warming box. Unheated, the church was built for some comfort in cold and drafty weather. Each pew had a metal plate identifying the family whose pew it was. Thus, we know that George Washington occupied a front row pew. A balcony at the back of the church was reserved for the students of the College of William and Mary. Here the initials

"T.J" have been found carved in a railing. We know that Thomas Jefferson attended the school there and many guess that he did the carving in the balcony at the Bruton Parish Church.

Reflecting briefly that his maternal grandfather had been a priest in the Church of England, Bob, for the moment, regretted that his parents had not stayed with this church. He then might have been invited to a close-up view of the Queen at worship on Sunday morning. Worshipers that Sunday were by invitation only. They were the prominant people of Williamsburg and some politicians. Instead, Bob walked around the grounds in the hope of seeing The Queen as she made a tour of the historic buildings. He stationed himself at the Palace steps along with other tourists. With a white handkerchief in hand, like his operatic idol Luciano Pavoratti, he hoped for a glimpse and a wave to royalty.

His moment of high drama came at about 2:00 p.m. when the carriage pulled up and a footman disembarked to aid the Queen to the pavement. She looked Bob's way with a faint smile and tilt of her head. He returned her smile with a bow and wave of his handkerchief. She turned and was gone, and that was all there was, but it made his day. Bob was not around for her return visit fifty years later, when she again stayed at the Inn and thrilled the people of Colonial Williamsburg and America by participating in the 400th Anniversary of the founding of the Colony of Jamestown.

Chapter 31

One day, he realized that the time had come for him to build again. This would be a house that he could think of as his and Rosa's retirement home. He knew that he would have next to nothing in retirement pay, not having put in enough years before retirement. After twenty-five years working for the Colonial Williamsburg Foundation his retirement pay would be fixed at only one hundred dollars a month. There would be no Social Security checks coming in as he had never paid into the system.

He couldn't depend on his painting restoration work to go on indefinitely.

He wanted Rosa to be secure if he should die before her and he needed a plan. He didn't want to end up working in a shoe store or department store in town, as some of his recently retired buddies from Colonial Williamsburg were doing to make ends meet. His father had taught him an important lesson when he gave him a whipping for leaving the rent money on a wall. What it meant to his parents when he went around, at the end of each month, collecting rents, became even more clear to him now. This would be the route he would take to his own security.

Bob could do for himself and his wife what his father had done for his family. Through rent money he would gain extra income each month. Bob had helped his father build some of their tenant houses in Metheun, Massachusetts and knew he owed his carpentry skills to him. Though he always held that his father was a tough old man-too tough on him at times-he respected him.

He would start with just a garage in which to store tools and lumber, then would proceed to building a barn, a house, a studio and a caretaker cottage. He had been saving money from the extra jobs and restoration work he was doing. He would purchase from the building material Mr. Rockefeller had provided to the employees from old houses that had to be torn down.

Everything that could be salvaged from the old houses was collected and labeled with a price as low as a quarter for a pound of drop nails, fifty cents for a window, a dollar for a door. Years later, the receipts Bob kept in his attic were interesting to read. He had paid two dollars for a door which must have been four inches thick of solid wood. It had a drop bar lock on the inside and forged steel hinges. The door jamb and framing came from the same historic house. This was Bob's front door. He would also purchase the materials for sale from the Navy baracks being torn down after the Second World War. These were mostly doors, windows and lumber.

He found a parcel of land halfway between historic Jamestown and Colonial Williamsburg on Neck-O-Land Road, an old coach road that, two hundred years earlier, went from Williamsburg to Jamestown and dead-ended at the James River. It still dead-ends there. This is where the historic Jamestown originally stood. It was moved to its present higher and drier location, perhaps in the 1930s, but never reconstructed completely as an historic village until the 1980s.

Bob's land was a generous looking acre of large old trees and undergrowth. It looked bigger because of the deep woods that ran along the back boundary and open fields on either side of it. It was big enough to accommodate the structures he had in mind and a comfortable distance from the few neighbors who had already built on Neck-O-Land Road.

On high ground, the adjacent acreage extended downward by at least ten acres to the James River. There, it dipped into swamp land, picking up an inlet of the James where small watercraft were moored. Through the James River a craft could travel a relatively short distance to the Chesapeake Bay. In the other direction, from his land, there were about five acres that bordered Jamestown Road. This road was the main throughway that went from Jamestown to the College of William and Mary and the Colonial Capital grounds. Neck-O-Land Road forked off this road and ended at the river.

Bob's acre, which he named 'Webb's Acre,' was high and dry. Even a portion of the lower ground down by the river was dry enough that a dairy farm prospered there. It would be a monumental job to clear the large trees on his property that were several feet in diameter. They stood where he wanted to build. A giant ash tree some five feet across occupied the place where he wanted to site his house! In time, he would win this battle of the woods, with help from his right hand man, "Shorty," the nickname all gave to Harvey Johnson, his shop maintenance man, who stood about five foot three inches tall. Incidentally, Shorty's daughter also worked for the Foundation in the kitchen of the Inn. According to Bob, she baked the finest pastries to be had anywhere. Shorty was a good family man and a loyal friend. He stood by his friend through years of grounds work and the building to follow, on Webb's Acre.

Hours and days of backbreaking work had produced a clearing of trees and brush. More than once Bob thought surely he had ruined his old truck by forcing it to pull stumps from the ground. In the end, it was he and Shorty who had all but broken their own backs! What they couldn't pull out they hacked out. What couldn't be hacked, they tried dousing with gasoline and burning out. They dug, used hatchets, axes, a chain saw, shovels. They probably chased more snakes, skunks, raccoons and rabbits back to the woods than they would ever see again. In the end, Bob had to pay to have someone come and haul away all the debris unearthed, but his ground was cleared.

One party favorite story was that while they were working close together in a trench they had just dug Bob had leaned on his shovel and exclaimed, "Shorty, you smell like an old polecat." Shorty shot back, "Mr. Webb, you don't smell like no sweet smellin' rose youself." They worked well together and would continue to do so to the end. Both retired together and continued working Webb's Acre as it grew and changed. Even when completed, the grass always needed mowing.

Chapter 32

Williamsburg, guarded by being far enough inland from the bay, was perfectly positioned between the two rivers, the James and the York, to avoid hurricane force storms, though they had been known to happen. The rivers would swell, but seldom exceed their banks. Shingles and signs would get twisted and a bonnet from an historic maiden would go flying, but major damage seldom occurred.

One day, as Bob was working in the paint shop, wind whistled around the windows and bent the evergreens nearly to the ground. The rain pelted so hard on the windowpane, he thought it surely would break. When it bounced off in little pellets and skittered across the parking lot, he knew this was a real storm. It was fierce, and the new paint he had just put on the restored Powell-Waller House was in jeapardy. A light cool rain would do no harm however, and he was sure it had a "skin" on it already. He hoped there would be no ill affect by the heavy gale. His hope was realized with no damage done.

Fortunately, the weather held out till he had finished the garage on Neck-O-Land Road. The old lumber from the stock for sale at Colonial Williamsburg had just been placed there. It was heart pine to be used for the flooring in his new house. Of random widths, it would be a little more difficult to lay, but more interesting to look at. Some widths were as much as ten and twelve inches.

The ferocious storm was short lived; about twenty minutes. Then, a beautiful rainbow arched over the whole historic village from the Governors Palace at one end to the George Wythe house at the other, on the grounds of the College of William and Mary. Bob called to his shop maintenance man, "Shorty," to close up shop, it was time to go home to Neck-O-Land Road.

When they arrived at Webb's Acre, they found that it had rained in the one garage window which had been left open, as the windup mechanism never quite came all the way closed. Bob felt they could blame the Navy for that, since this was one of the surplus windows he had bought in Newport News when they tore down the old Navy barracks. The boards they had stored to build the house had gotten soaked due to the ill fitting window.

With foresight Bob had created a large asphalt parking area to the right of the garage and he and Shorty dragged the boards out and laid them flat on this pavement to dry. Trusting that it would not rain again, or if it did, it couldn't do any more harm, they left them there for several days, turning them daily so as to keep them from warping. No more rain came, and in time they dried straight and firm. The garage window got fixed and the boards went back in for storage.

Bob next turned his attention to building a small outbuilding to accommodate all the tools and paraphanalia needed for carpentry work. The garage was not enough. He also had in mind the need to lock up such items. In the future, this new building would also be a storage unit for paintings from the Abbey Aldridge Folk Art Museum, of the C.W. Foundation. Mary Black, Director, had asked him to continue to do the restoration of some paintings and wood carvings from the collection. Bob was happy for the extra work and extra pay. He also liked to keep his hand in this skill he had learned from a master restorer in Sarasota, Florida.

With his usual thought for the future Bob had in mind from the beginning that this new structure would some day become another rental cottage. He called it a mini barn. When finished it was just big enough to convert to a living room, bedroom, kitchen, bath and screened porch. An old horse collar was acquired from somewhere and hung at the kitchen entrance door. A large wagon wheel stood on the other side of the door. The barn was painted red, of course. As a real barn, it had vertical slats running from ground to roof with a cupola and weather vane on the roof. It set a precedent for charm that the next three houses would live up to in their own unique ways. One would be a caretaker cottage, another his painting studio, and years later a third was simply called "The Wheel House" made just for what it was, a rental cottage.

Chapter 33

The main house, the Webb's future home, was the third and most demanding undertaking. Many nights and weekends were spent on this. When it finally came to putting the shingles on the roof, Bob experienced the same problem he had encountered in New Jersey. He had to work at night and disturb the neighborhood. These neighbors were not so tolerant as others had been, and called the sheriff. The sheriff in this part of Virginia covered problems in the rural areas. Bob was on the roof and kept working while telling the sheriff he was nearly done pounding and if the officer would lay down his gun, pick up a hammer and climb up to help him, he would be done in no time flat. The sheriff stood around talking and listening for far longer than he would normally have, thus allowing Bob time to finish the job. Bob came down and offered him a drink but, on duty yet, the sheriff refused, accepting a soft drink instead and engaging in light conversation until he finally had to leave.

Over the years the home got added to and changed several times. From the beginning however, the plan was for the house to have a country charm with an oversized fireplace and iron kettles that would swing on an arm. When a storm would interrupt rural electricity, the Webb's cooking was done in iron pots over the fire. A hand pump was installed in the backyard which was of service when there was no power; an occurance of several times a year! Some years later Bob built a smokehouse and in the cold months had bacon hanging there. A shed behind the garage held tools. This was later converted to a chicken coop.

Many thought Webb's Acre reminded them of a little 18th Century village or a miniature Colonial Williamsburg. This would be reasonable as the men who helped build it were the same carpenters, and craftsmen who built Colonial Williamsburg. Bob and Shorty did not do it alone. These men helped each other in the early days when they were anxious to have homes of their own.

They traded skills in a barter system whereby each gave to the others according to his skill. Bob, of course was the painter but could do other carpentry tasks and worked where he was needed. There was a licensed electrcian, a plumber, cement man to make slabs and steps, and a landscaper. An architect took Bobs ideas and drafted plans to be submitted to the County Planning Commission for approval. Everything was done according to building codes. They applied for and got building permits which Bob proudly hammered to a tree within sight of all. At each phase of the completion, city or county inspectors were called in and approved the work.

The men liked working together. They appreciated that sometimes Bob had to travel long distances to their locations. Some had chosen to build their homes across one of the rivers or on the other side of Williamsburg from Neck-O-Land Road. He worked on weekends and didn't mind the travel. Those helping him usually came directly from work. The distance was short as Neck-O-Land Road was only three miles from the Colonial Capital. In the end all felt they had given and received an equal share in services. They remained good friends and continued to help one another down through the years.

Bob's day job was demanding, but he never missed getting done what he had to do. He used his varied skills to add such enhancements to the historic village as marbleized arches and entranceways in the Williamsburg Inn and marbleized fireplaces in some of the houses. He liked to point out that everything done at Colonial Williamsburg was a cooperative effort of many individuals. No one person alone could take credit for anything completed – least of all, himself.

Chapter 34

With most of the construction work on Webb's Acre completed, Bob had reached retirement age and, with Rosa, was happy to settle into living as they pleased on their little 'estate.' There were a few things he wanted yet to make it complete. He would have to have a kitchen garden, a farm animal, chickens possibly, and two or three rows of grape vines for making wine. The terrain was such that each of these goals was possible. It would take time, but, with retirement, he had plenty of that. He would continue to hire his shop maintanence man from the paint shop, who had retired with him. The city bus traveled the route of the black community and picked up city workers dropping them off at the bus station where Bob met Shorty each day. He would return him there at the end of their work day to catch the bus for home.

Shorty sometimes got tired on the job but found ways of looking busy-feeling he had to earn his pay- he would occasionally take the lawnmower apart and put it back together! He would half fall off his stool as he slept through the work day. Bob understood and left him alone on those days he didn't feel like working. Shorty wouldn't think of staying home, however. The truth was, both men wanted to continue their routine of daily work as long as they could.

The gully was far enough away from the house that Bob thought he could keep a farm animal down there. It seemed a proper place for a pig. They would build a stye. When it rained the hog would enjoy wallowing in the deluge that naturally flowed through the gully. It could easily be fed each day with grain and scraps from the garden and table. He would buy a pigglet from a local farmer when a sow produced a litter in the spring.

In the meantime Bob called a carpenter from Colonial Williamsburg who liked working on weekends to earn a little extra money. He was not one of the original barter team and was a rather peculiar fellow. Tall, lean and bronzed, with chiseled features and long straight black hair, he looked like what he was, a Native American. He walked with such a stealth manner, unfortunately, people were suspicious of him. The women in the neighborhood didn't like his disrespectful manner of referring to his wife as "the sqaw." Bob liked him because he followed instructions and worked quietly with little to say. He could depend on him to show up and get a job done. Together they built the shed and the smokehouse.

With this done, word came from the farmer that a piglet was ready to be picked up. Bob prepared a wooden crate with some straw and a lid that could be wired closed and drove out to pick up his little pink, curly tailed piglet. It had been weaned from its mother and was ready to start on a regular diet.

The pig would one day be a hog and ready for butchering. Bob had to give him a name that would make that job easier for him. He didn't want to become attached to it as a pet. Therefore he called him 'The Major'. The Major must have been a most dispictable individual to merit such a destiny and be so disliked by Bob who wasn't known to dislike anyone. People's actions may have displeased him but he never discarded anyone as an individual.

Before The Major became bacon however, he

enjoyed a lazy life of just eating and getting fat. He got so big and cumbersome that one day in moving around his stall he misstepped and hit a rail, breaking it. An opening was created and out he went sauntering into the woods. The woods backed up on all the properties and was quite deep. It went lengthwise all the way to the James River. The Major blissfully grunted and rooted through the brush feasting on all that hogs like to feast on.

Bob went down to the pen at noon to 'slop' his hog and discovered that The Major had escaped. He knew he had to be in the woods and not too far away and figured it would take a posse' of at least five men to help round him up and drive him back to his pen. Fortunately it was a Saturday and Bob went around the neighborhood gathering volunteers and was able to salicit a college of William and Mary professor who lived down the road and his son who was a lawyer. Two college students, who were also his tenants thought it would be great fun and joined him to make up the body of five bent on capturing the wayward hog.

They soon caught wind of him and could hear him grunting blissfully. Each man had a stick and proceeded to surround him, intent on driving him back to his pen. The Major had other ideas and escaped, dashing deeper into the woods where there was water. He entered the shallow stream, and flopped down, rolling over. The Neck-O-Land Posse' brigade caught up with him and Bob began giving orders. He sent the two students to the garage and shed to bring back a rope and a ladder for binding and transporting the hog.

What a sight to see these 20th century men looking for all the world like aboriginese hunters emerging from the woods with their catch secured and hanging down between two bearers at the front and two at the rear of the ladder. They were wet, muddy, and disheveled , and laughing hilariously. The women in the neigborhood stood in Bob's parking lot looking bewildered by this scene. The Major met his demise shortly thereafter and the new smokehouse was put to it's first use. Bob's one experience as a hog farmer was enough. The story of the wayward pig would live in neighborhood lore.

In years to come the Webbs would make a day of it and cross the river, on a ferry to Surry where they would have lunch and buy sixty pounds of bacon at a processing farm curing Virginia Hams and other pork products. The company always added a bucket of hickory chips for the smoking. Working on a table in the garage Bob used Mortons Curing Salt and brown sugar, working it well into the meat. He then cut lengths of three foot slabs. These were pounded onto metal forks and hoisted up, by a pole, onto pegs in the smokehouse. A twist of the pole and the fork, holding the bacon, was released onto the peg. The smokehouse was filled with hanging slabs ready to receive smoke from the hickory fire below. A small fire would be built on the ground and stoked to stay burning through three days and two nights.

At Christmas time the neighbors looked forward to seeing smoke curling from the rafters of the smokehouse, and smelling the hickory smoke as it drifted far and wide. This meant a slab of bacon for each. Bob always had enough to go around and would send a slab to his brother, Arthur, in Florida.

Chapter 35

$\mathcal{S}$hortly after his retirement, Bob had the opportunity to accept an overwhelming artistic challenge. When a flood in Venice, Italy threatened to ravish the great masterworks of the Renaissance, the Italian government asked for world help. They called for conservators from the industrial nations to help. Not only were skilled craftsmen needed, but also money, lots of it, to meet guest workers' living expenses as well as for materials to do the job. America responded with many celebrities in the arts taking this as their personal call to be charitable. They went on radio and television asking private citizens for financial cotributions, while donating their own time to the cause.

The Ringling Museum, as most museums

across the country, was asked to offer names of conservators who would be interested in helping. The Director of the Ringling Museum talked to Bob and learned he would be willing to go to Italy for a limited time. Two personalities came forth volunteering to appear on television with a craftsman and explain the need of the publics support. Thus Bob was chosen to appear on national television with Richard Burton and Elizabeth Taylor !

He was asked afterwards by friends if Elizabeth Taylor was as beautiful up close and in person as she was in the movies. "Yes indeed, of course !" he exclaimed. "Her most remarkable feature was her eyes. They were an amazing mixture of green-gray, lavender and blue." Which was the striking observation of the color artist Bob Webb.

Bob went to flood-ravished Italy and was immediately given a cadre of craftsmen to organize. After an overview of the situation, he concluded that total restoration of the many masterpieces was nearly impossible because there was such tremendous water damage. It would take a lifetime to restore all the damaged art works, if it were possible to restore them at all. He felt that the answer for the saving of future works rested with engineers.

Engineers would have to eventually design

some system to hold back the natural flooding which occurs regularly in this part of Italy. Bob spent considerable time doing what he could to get the work started and moving forward. He then enjoyed what little time off they could take exploring Italy.

As a place to live while there, he was given a room in a private home. On first entering his room, he noticed a window box with straw in it on the sill. He wondered what it was about but it didn't take long to find out. Suddenly there was a flutter of feathers, and a hen lighted in the box! Bob was delighted. The hen sat there and Bob sat down to watch her. Very shortly he heard a cackle through the window pane, and he knew what that ment. She had laid an egg!

To retrieve an egg from a sitting hen was no new experience for the farm boy now painting restorer. First he had to open the window, then very quietly and very gently he would flatten out his hand and go under the hen. With thumb and index finger he would encircle the egg and gently pull it back and out. Success ! With delight, he went in search of the mistress of the house and presented her with this gift. Neither could speak the other's language, and they resorted to pantomime. She communicated that the egg would be for Bobs breakfast in the morning. He thought what a gracious way of making a stranger feel at home.

The time came for him to leave and he left with regret that he could do so little to solve their problems. Though he was asked to stay and supervise more of the project, he had his wife at home and his own work to do. He had done his best to organize the work and felt it could go on without him. The international conservationists had made a good start and this was all that could reasonably be expected of them. The Italians would have to solve their flooding problem and he felt they would, after so nearly a total disaster. He very much wanted them to, as the great paintings of the Renaissance had inspired him to his life's work. It would be a shame for new generations to lose this great heritage.

In leaving Italy, he had a very good feeling about the people. He had learned that the Italians were warm and generous, fun loving and they could cook! These were qualities he liked about the Italians and he knew he couldn't stay away, he would be back. He did come back later and brought his two daughters with him. At another time he brought his teenage grandson. With the Italians, as with 'Bobo Webbo', that's what they called him, the love affair was mutual. He would always be welcomed.

He headed home to Williamsburg, Virginia to be with his wife whom he felt he had been away from too long. He had a barn full of paintings to be restored. Arriving in time to enjoy the beautiful magnolia tree in full bloom, he felt he was lucky to have all that he had here on Webb's Acre. The grass had been newly mowed and he knew that Shorty had taken care of the grounds while he was gone. He was fortunate to have a tenant like Henry who had driven him to the airport and now picked him up.

As they pulled over in front of the garage doors the sound of crunching acorns was a sure sign of fall. The big oak tree by the chimney rained down hundreds of them. The property had many holly trees that were also in their full regalia of red berries. Bob knew that the fig tree behind the house would be loaded with ripe fruit. The red and pink peonies that bordered the property where in bloom. Tiger lilies lined the driveway and made a circle around the birdbath near his studio window. All this was a panorama of beauty Bob was proud of. He was home and happy to be back.

Chapter 36

Another job after his retirement, had been recommended by Mr Chorley, his old C.W. boss. It was for the restoration of the Old Salem Colonial Village in Winston Salem, North Carolina. Bob had not done any of the original work there, but because of the recommendation he took the job. He was in his mid-sixties and still in top physical condition. Confident about working on a scaffold, he trusted that the corporate management of Old Salem would have a crew of men capable of erecting one correctly.

Bob mounted the scaffold and climbed some eight feet up. When he turned to secure his equipment tray, the entire structure shifted. The footing catwalk on which he was standing tilted, throwing him the eight feet down to the hard floor below. They had apparently failed to secure some part of the mechanism to hold it in place. Bob was confined to the hospital in Winston Salem, North Carolina, for some days with five broken ribs.

The situation was even more serious because his ailing wife was with him in a motel. Bob had wanted her to come along as she was a native of North Carolina and they planned to visit her relatives in a few days. He no longer had a full time aide-companion for her. Their friends, Floyd and his wife, came to their aid, hurrying to Winston Salem to stay with Rosa, and finally bring the two of them back to Williamsburg.

The old Salem Village was a living museum in a much smaller dimension than that of Colonial Williamsburg. Bob felt that this state supported North Carolina Corporation should compensate him for his broken ribs, lost time, and lost income from restoration work he had to do at home; as well as for what it had done to his domestic life. They didn't seem to think they owed him anything! He finally decided to sue them and his legal argument went from the lower court to the federal court. This was possible as Bob was not a citizen of North Carolina and therefore could appeal to the Federal Court, in this case against the state.

The tangle Bob found himself in was about as painful as the many broken ribs he had suffered. Since he was working on his own, and not as one loaned by Mr. Rockefeller, or anyone else, it was up to him to get his own lawyer and formally make a claim for compensation. This was his first on the job injury and he had to learn how to handle it. He was not seeking a workmens compensation-not being eligiable for it; but simply wanted to be paid for his loses. He was retired and had no social security, never having paid into it. He had medical insurance, but felt that Old Salem owed him for additional pain and suffering and medical expenses not covered. His travel time, motel stays, and other costs were significant.

After recuperating, Bob brought his own lawyer to North Carolina and presented his case. The judge said he found it all very interesting and would need to hear more before making a judgement. He required him to come back to court many times. After getting over his frustration, Bob rather enjoyed the trips back to North Carolina and his day, or days, in court. His lawyer, who was also his next door neighbor, allowed him to do most of the talking. Bob was good at that and enjoyed presenting his own case in his own style. He injected enough humor, balanced with the seriousness of the situation that it became a first rate performance, drawing an encore from the judge! He wanted Bob to come back in a month and they would go over it again.

Periodically, over a ten year period, Bob and his lawyer were called back to North Carolina to appear before the same judge each time ! It seems that the judge may have been enjoying Bob Webb as much or more than the case itself ! This was what his attorney reported. Finally, after ten years, the judge was about to retire and awarded Bob ten thousand dollars. He then closed the case.

The governor of North Carolina heard about the case and took an interest in it and in Bob Webb. For several years after that, he found reasons to make trips to Williamsburg and while there visited the Webbs on Neck-O-Land Road. Some of Bob's friends met the governor at Bobs home and confirmed this to be true. Bob frequently told stories that people doubted because they seemed so implausible. Eventually, something or someone, would substantiate them. More than one person said they had met the governor when he came to visit the Webbs at their home.

Chapter 37

Webb's Acre continued to develope with the planting of enough grape-vines to allow for sufficient wine after several years of growth. Trellis were erected and ground turned for planting concord grapes back by the woods. Bob found tenants he liked and kept the rents low so they would stay. Some lived there for years, leaving only when they got married and needed more space. One young man, Henry, felt guilty that he had lived there for so many years and his rent had never been raised. He decided to raise it himself! Henry had been a good tenant and helper to Bob. Sometimes he would drive the Webbs to Florida in their car and Bob would pay for his ticket to fly home again. He did many small things to be of help and Bob, though happy for him regretted losing such a good tenant and friend when he got married and left Webb's Acre.

Bob continued to make trips to the Rockefeller kitchen and learn from the cook over there. He kept up his skills in cooking and after acquiring new recipes calling for the use of herbs and spices, he experimented by trying them out. Of course one day every two weeks was spent baking bread. Bob had installed an eight foot long solid maple counter top in the kitchen which was ideal for bread preparation. He could roll out one long coil of dough-the length of the counter- and cut it into six or eight loaves. The oven was kept busy for hours. Lucky tenants and friends were always the recipients of this bounty.

Life was full with the only thorn being the demon that caused Rosa to shake and fall. Her condition was gradually getting worse and their children were becoming concerned for their father; the caretaker, as well. His health was good but Rosas condition was more and more demanding. He wanted to continue to be her only caregiver but his daughters felt differently.

Bob never wanted to give up Rosa but finally, after years and dwindling energy as well as patience, he allowed for her to be admitted to a nursing home in New Jersey, where Thelma was living. A very short time after that he got a call from his daughter asking him to come right away. Her mother was failing and would not last much longer. Bob had asked his friend, Floyd, to drive with him to New Jersey and when they were within five miles of the hospital Bob had a sense that there was no point in hurrying; she was gone. He looked at his watch and when they arrived at the hospital he learned she had died at just that same time. He went to her bedside and closed the curtain and spent considerable time alone with her. He then left and he and Floyd drove all the way back to Williamsburg. His daughters carried out the prearrangements they all had made.

Needing to be settled in his mind in order to paint, Bob stopped painting. He was not settled. His routine had been built around his wife and now there were no demands on him. Always doing everything himself around the property, independant of Rosa, he thought he should be able to carry on as usual but he could not. He made the rounds of visiting many friends in Williamsburg, but soon tired of that. Nothing he did would raise his spirits.

He decided to have a party for his tenants in which they could invite whomever they chose. The violin player who played at the Williamsburg Inn dinning room, would be invited to entertain them. It would be a cookout where he would have steaks over a backyard grill. This took a lot of preparation and his tenant, Henry, helped him. Everyone enjoyed the party but when it was over Bob found himself once again facing lonliness and his lose. It had only served as a high from which he now had a terrible hangover.

When winter came he tried to continue hs life as before by going back to Sarasota, Florida and working on the Ringling mansion, doing restoration of his own original work. His heart was no longer in it. Indeed this would be the last trip he would make to Florida. Some said that while in Florida he lived a wild life of debauchery with loose women, and drinking! He spent money and gave it away as if it were water flowing through an opened dam, until finally he had had enough of such living. Probably out of money, he packed up and went home to Williamsburg. Later, from home in Williamsburg, he sold his trailor by telephone, thus permanently breaking his tie to Sarasota. All that was in the trailor, including many of his paintings, went with the sale. They were as a gift.

When spring came, he knew he needed life around him and would try to think of ways to bring people to Webb's Acre. His old friends were loyal and almost daily someone stopped by to visit him. It wasn't enough. He felt as if he should be doing something but he didn't know what. He was forever poised for some action he didn't need to take. Rosie no longer needed such vigilance, but he couldn't let go.

From the very beginning, he had put one large mailbox at the end of the drive in which all the tenants' mail was placed by the postman. Each tenant came to the main house to collect his mail from Bob. They were all young men at that time and Bob enjoyed these daily brief visits with them. The mail situation was a good plan for both tenants and Bob.(They were like his sons and helped to ease his pain.)The mailbox only became an issue later when women had either moved in with the men or rented on their own. They wanted their privacy and speed in collecting their mail after a day of work or classes.

With the cultural change, Bob had let go of his lease requirement that single men and single women could not live together. He simply had to work it out as to who would pay the rent if one moved out. He arranged that only one of the party would sign the lease and be responsible. This new way of living was not easy for Bob to accept but he had to change when he found that his lease was increasingly unenforceable.

Another idea for getting people to visit him

was to put a "FOR SALE' sign out at the end of the drive. He didn't intend to sell the property but enjoyed talking to the few prospective buyers who would stop by. His daughter, Thelma, decided this was not such a good idea. Bob felt she had begun to take too much interest in his life and he blamed himself for giving up many of his own interests. Yet he knew he had to allow himself time to be distracted. Distractions had been neccessary until he could return to his work and responsibilities. Summer slipped into fall.

He walked down the drive to the mailbox, expecting that the mail carrier had been there and left a bundle of letters. The letters he carried back made his step feel lighter as he thought about their importance to his tenants. He had a duty to them to deliver their mail. There were other responsibilities he had to his tenants and to himself so that Webb's Acre might keep going.

It was October and he and Shorty needed to prepare the plants for winter. He needed to caulk around the windows of the main house. He needed to run an add in the newspaper for a new tenant, as the law student living in the Cottage with his wife would be moving out. He had passed his bar exams and got a good job with a prestigious company in Richmond. Bob had seen little of them since they moved in two years previous. It seemed that they worked and studied all the time. He would remember to wish them luck before they left. He knew he would be all right now. He was returning to himself.

Chapter 38

$\mathcal{A}$lthough he had only a sixth grade education, Robert Webb was sharp and he kept his rental properties maintained and solvent. He kept detailed records of each house and tenant with rents and expenses recorded. Interestingly these were kept in hard bound ledger books, each of a different bright color and with a painted picture of the particular house it recorded. Each book showed the history of that house with its transactions and changes of tenants.

He did his own tax work, keeping track of expense receipts for every expenditure. When there were vacancies, he ran adds in the Virginia Gazette and interviewed people, having in mind that he wanted tenants who would take care of the property. He had an effective lease that protected himself and at once defined perimeters for the tenant. At times, tenants would be asked to leave for some small infraction. Renting these charming little houses was not difficult and he made no allowance for the slightest infraction of the lease.

At times he would have an especially difficult tenant who did not pay his rent on time, or was distructive, or was using the house for other than a place to live. If he refused to leave Bob would take him to court. He would present the case himself before the judge and would nearly always win. He had an uncanny sense for smelling out trouble. At times he could make mistakes in judging character but soon discovered and rectified his error.

He allowed a certain young man to move in without furniture or even any sign of clothing! This fellow would go out only at night and stay locked up in the Barn-the rental house, in the daytime. His behavior was not normal and Bob was suspicious of him. He entered his house, which he could do according to the lease, and found what appeared to be narcotics there! He immediately called the police who arrived in about five minutes flat. The young man, who had just come home before they arrived and Bob were having an argument about Bob entering his house, when the police arrived. The two officers were overjoyed to have caught him! Apparently he had escaped from jail or prison and had seen the ad in the paper for this rental ! Bob became more careful in his interviewing after that.

His housekeeper, Virginia was now retired, though his yard man, Shorty, still came and mowed the grass. At times they both needed and accepted his help. Bob, like Mr Ringling, had a paternal interest in his help that didn't end with their retirement. Neither were receiving Social Security. Shortys' retirement pay from C.W. was probably even lower than Bob's meager one hundred dollars a month.

Virginia had been their housekeeper for years. She was an interesting genetic mixture of backgrounds. The Native Americans throughout the tidewater had been there since the settlers first came. Some escaped the long march west to incampments on reservations. The few that remained on the coast intermarried with Englishmen, Germans, and freed slaves. Generations later, Bob thought Virginia to be the offspring of such mixture. She carried features of high cheekbones, dark skin, and cobalt blue eyes. Her hair was coal black, and she wore it straight.

Virginia worked many years for the five or six families on Neck-O-Land Road, doing their cooking, housekeeping, and helping with the children as they came along and grew up. She also worked for several Colonial Williamsburg employees. She did a great deal in the care of Rosa and Bob frequently asked her to work overtime when he had dinner parties or outdoor gatherings where he needed a server.

Aware that Virginia lived in a little shack in an overgrown field at the edge of town, and without electricity or running water-she used a little stream running through the lot- he bought a hand pump and had it put in her yard. He provided her with a castiron cookstove which would also supply heat. Bob said he had to work clandestinely to get these things installed. He hired black laborers to do the work at night, because many people would not approve of "a white's intrusion into a black's lifestyle," he stated. This was the south and some still carried old ideas and the old "southern thoughts," he would say.

He frequently helped Shorty when his family responsibilities got too heavy. Bob was good at saving money and more than once strangers and friends alike came to him for loans to help them over a hump. These loans would be interest free and he said he was always paid back. From his early days with the circus, for him, banks continued to be suspect; consequently he kept rather large sums of cash on hand. Sometimes merchants would come to him for a 'fast loan' to pay for an incoming shipment on a Friday. On Monday they would repay him. Such loans were on a referral basis by good friends he trusted. He also had a gun and would not be afraid to use it if some thief, knowing he had money on the property, might choose to invade his house.

This does not mean he was wealthy. He gave away nearly all of his money after Rosas death. Bob's wish was to die with but a hundred dollars in his pocket as John Ringling had done! His wifes death was very hard for him and he must have thought life was finished for him as well! He would rebound. In another two or three years he would again come to know a sense of security, freedom and wellbeing he had not known for many years.

The time came when Virginia could no longer make the rounds of working for the families on Neck-O-Land Road and Bob had to find another cook-housekeeper. He was a good cook but soon tired of making the effort for three meals a day. And housekeeping was totally out of his 'pay scale.' It had been almost three years that he had been alone. He needed a helper and decided to advertise in the newspaper. Before doing that he had called and put his name in to receive deliveries of "Meals on Wheels."

It amused him that a number of those delivering meals were elderly widows "with an eye out for an eligable widower, " he said. They treated him royally, bringing him fancy deserts he knew were not a part of the menu, but he couldn't be interested in any of them-the deliverers that is. He looked carefully at those who answered his ads but again he was not enamored by any of them. It was obvious that he was searching for more than a cook-houskeeper.

CHAPTER 39

here was one helper who told him she knew of a young woman that he might like to meet. Just because the two of them were artists and would have a lot to talk about, she felt they should get together. She offered to do the cooking if Bob would invite this lady to have dinner at his home. This was an art therapist working at the same hospital where the 'matchmaker' helper also worked part- time. Bob said, "why not?" and the lady, when asked also said, "why not?'

It was a rather atypical date in that after Bob called Kathy and invited her to dinner he gave her directions as to how to get to his house! It seemed strange that he wasn't going to pick her up at her apartment but that was all right with her. artists are known to do things differently, she thought. She liked this arrangement, because it seemed easier to get into her own car and leave early if she was so inclined.

It was dark when Kathy arrived and pitch dark on Webb's Acre. Her headlights found the parking lot behind the modest little stuco cottage set well back from the road, off a long driveway. Because the yard was dark, this was all she could see at the end of the drive dimly lit by a single pole lamp. Her host was at the back steps to meet her. He appeared to be tall, self-possessed and a distinguished looking gentleman, with neatly combed white hair, and perhaps in his sixties. Her co-worker, the cook was right behind him waving and bidding her to come in. She noted that the kitchen was the main entrance to the house! This is where the parking lot was and the front door was dark and remote and without parking facilities. It's only function later, would be as entrance to a newly attached screened porch.

Dinner went well and the conversation was so lively and interesting neither were aware that the cook had gone home. 1:00 a.m. came and Kathy was still there ! They hadn't left the dinningroom table; so engrossed were they in their talk and with each other. Another hour went by before

Bob walked her to her car and they embraced and kissed goodnight. He handed her one of his little paintings, not sure whether he would ever see her again; and he wanted her to remember him. He then did ask her when he might see her again! They arranged for a date the following week in which he would come to her apartment to pick her up. She went home and that same night wrote to a friend stating that she had met the most exciting, interesting, and attractive man she had ever known in her life and she knew she wanted to marry him.

There were two things he did not tell her the truth about himself. One was his age. She would learn later that he had taken off ten years which she accepted as about right for his age. She believed him. He also confided that he was "a man of means," as he phrased it. She had to laugh at this. He was so transparent and obviously not telling the truth. His expression or something in his eyes gave him away. She knew that he could never convincingly lie to her. It didn't matter and she told him so. She confided that she had her own security! It was too bad he felt he had to say this. It was unnecessary... and not complementary. Her financial security was her own affair and she had her own lawyer that she would keep. Bobs richness was rather that of character and that's what made him attractive and endearing. She sensed that he was frugal. She knew he did have, and always would have, money enough to take care of himself. Their ages difference was a span of some twenty years. She could accept this.

For Kathy and Bob each proved to be what the other wanted. They were mature and knew what was required for each of them in a life partner. It was some months before they tied the knot in a religious ceramony in which good friends were best man and witness. Afterward they went to the Williamsburg Inn and had dinner in the evening. On that December 19th, the Inn was already festive with Christmas decorations. A second marriage for Bob, his first wife Rosa having died some three years previous, it was the first for Kathy.

CHAPTER 40

The following are random selections from the memoirs of Katheryn Webb, called Kathy.

Bob wanted to travel to an exotic place and we agreed that either Russia or China would be an exciting honeymoon trip. After much time in planning, though still early in our marriage, before chickens or a dog, we went to Russia.

We arrived in New Jersey by flight, and were met by Thelma who had just married her fourth husband, Walter. They seemed a happy couple and we were happy for them. They took us to the New York port where we would board our Russian cruise ship heading for ports in England, France, and Germany with time to spend a day in each place. The ship would also stop in Latvia,

Lithuania, and Estonia to let passangers off and pick others up.

Thelma took pictures of us as we stood on the dock before our towering ship carrying the flag of the hammer and sickle. On board, at the railing, we excitedly waved to them as our ship slipped out of its birth and away from our homeland. The Statue of Liberty receded behind us as we headed out to sea on this small Russian vessel. We learned later, unknown to any at the time, that the Mikhail Lermintov was a spy ship for the Soviets and it would be the last U.S.S.R. ship permitted into American ports during the cold-war! It was advertized as a cruise ship. Looking back, we still considered ourselves fortunate to have been able to visit Russia and the great art museum The Hermitage in Leningrad, now St. Petersburg.

We hadn't known what it ment to live under communism but soon found out. On board we were told we would be living as Communist and that our eighteen days cruise would give us a picture of the superiority of the Soviet Socialist form of government! We hadn't expected, nor did we care about such enlightenment. Our fellow passengers were mostly south Floridians with a few from New York, City. They all seemed to know each other. We were the only Virginians.

We were assigned seats in the dinning room, and were told to stay where assigned. No one would be permitted to come in late, even by five minutes! The doors would then be locked! We were on time and the doors were locked that first night. How could this be so superior to democracy?

Being American, none of the tourists could be disciplined to the Communist regime. We were aware that student servers had the dual role of also entertaining us with song and dance in the evenings. Thinking to help them, Bob and I sat where assigned the first evening. Our table partner immediately lit up a big cigar and puffed a cloud of smoke our way. We got up and moved. Others got up all over the dinning room and began seeking out their friends to sit with. The servers were beside themselves. Pandemonium ensued. They immediately ran to the kitchen seeking orders as to what to do.

The next day the problems were fixed. The doors were left open long enough for stragglers. We could sit where we pleased and discipline gave way to a more relaxed spirit. We learned that our captain had been educated in the U.S. and himself had intervened to solve the problems. He probably understood that those used to freedom couldn't be bolted down. Bob had a way with the young help and when language became a problem he endeared himself to them with pantomine laced with humor. He probably learned this from the clowns in Ringling's circus.

As an artist, Bob decided to bring along a small painting to give to the captain as a gesture of good will. In our stateroom we wrote a note making the offer, knowing that these people were strong on protocal. We got no answer for the whole trip to Lenengrad ! However, events took a turn once arriving at the Hermitage Museum.

Although in August, it started to snow as we waited in a long line outside the entrance. This was unexpected as was the confusing incident that occurred while we waited. I turned to talk to someone and in turning back Bob was gone! Looking back down the line thinking he had made good what he said about going to the bus-- because of the weather-- I didn't see him. Looking ahead, there he was being escorted, by a uniformed officer, into the Hermitage! I immediately broke from line and chased after them only to be caught by a matron, also in uniform who, with the strength of a bull, bodily liftted me from the pavement and dragged and pushed me back to my place in line!

"Nit!Nit!" she shouted. as I submitted to her superior strength and threat of a a whole bregade of such female force in uniform around her. I obediantly stood in line, alone and worried, waiting to move to the entrance. Bob was politically astute and I knew he had said nothing wrong. He projected warmth and good humor in any langwage. I was bewildered and just wanted to be with him. Without an enterpreter I could not ask the "nit,nit" matron or anyone else what had happened. There was nothing to do but wait and follow the line as it inched forward.

Chapter 41

Finally entering the museum, Bob was nowhere in sight and efforts to communicate were futile. I wandered down one gallery corridor after another while only stealing a glance at the gorgeous paintings everywhere. The rest of our group was already somewhere off into a guided tour and I went searching for Bob. Then over a loud speaker, in Russian I heard, "Katerina Vebb, Katerina Vebb, come to the entrance immediately." The foreign sound of my name took a minute to register that it was me they were addressing. I retraced to the entrance and there sat Bob with a big grin on his face and motioning me to sit down beside him. He said,"we've been invited to have lunch with the museum director and the chief painting conservator in fifteen minutes."

I was amazed, yet chagrined, and wanted to know why I had been so rudely handled and ignored. Bob said the director had apologized saying they didn't know I was with him. This was a communications problem, he stated. The museum officials, over lunch, were very warm to me however, showing interest in my professional background while expressing pride in their own women's accomplishments. One of their own had just been the first woman astronaut in space.

There seemed to have been a lot of communications about us before we got here! They knew all about us; that Bob had worked in Florida at the John and Mable Ringling Museum, he had been in the Navy; and that I was an alumni of the School of the Art Institute of Chicago and had taught at a mid-western college. How they knew so much and how or why we got this invitation we would never know. We didn't ask and conversation went smoothly over borsch and pickled fish. We delighted in a hot cup of tea.

We had several days of touring the old capital of Russia, Leningrad, and visiting Katherine the Great's summer palace. They took us to homes of several of their poets. Visits to the cathedrals were sad in that the desecration had been so complete. Icons had been removed and many sold in foreign markets. Interiors were ransacked and gutted, and the cathedrals were now being called museums. We felt a deep sympathy for the people on the streets and in the shops who were obviously poor, hungry, and without the modern amenities we were so used to. We found them, as well as our crew, to be warm, loving of their families, and with the basic values people share everywhere who live and work together.

Back on board ship we were invited to dinner at the captain's table. I had the honored position of being right of Alexander Borodin, Captain of the Mikhail Lermantov. The large golden cavier was delicious. I regret not asking Captain Boradin if he was related to the famous composer by the same name. We learned he had been retired but was asked to captain this ship for one last voyage. Before the trip was over we would be happy to have such an experienced man at the helm. He expressed that his wife was very sad that he was called back into service. He had to leave her alone in their dacha. The captain spoke very little English but Bob seemed comfortable in conversation with him talking mostly about their Navies and the great wars in which both men had served.

After dinner the chief officers and Bob were

lined up at the dinningroom entrance for picture taking. I was very proud of Bob as he stood in the middle of these officers, holding his painting which was a small oil of a red sunset. They had finally accepted it as a gift to the Russian Navy! All of this attention had a downside, however. With furtive glances our way, we sensed that our fellow tourists were suspicious of us; perhaps even thinking we were communist and Russian spys...so much attention was paid to us ! None of the tourists would speak to us after that. We knew no other passengers and had no time to explain-- if we could have-- as we just then ran into a cyclone at sea and were all confined to our cabins.

A few of us ventured to the dinning room each day and I brought back meals for Bob. They would not allow anyone able to go to the dinningroom, to take food out for themselves however, thus leaving me to share only a crust of bread with my husband. We who could, had to eat in the dinning room even though nothing would stay on the tables-- the tossing was so violent. Bob was somehow able to anchor his food and eat one morsel at a time.

Neither Bob nor I got seasick throughout the violent storm; however, walking through corridors was trecherous. Interestingly, chairs had hooks on the bottom and a chain that was then hooked to a latch on the floor, thus preventing them from flying about. At times waves engulfed our ship and from our window we could see the bottom of a wave and the water above passing over the top of us. The captain had cut the motor and allowed the ship to drift with the storm. It creked and jolted, rose and fell, bent over and righted itself for five days until we were just outside New York; then it calmed down.

How happy we were to see the Statue of Liberty! Our hearts filled with pride and love for our country. New York was beautiful with an early morning pink glow. Bob, with our luggage in each hand, pushed forward to the rail with me hanging on behind him. Everyone was pushing and shoving, aggressively eager to get off the ship and be back home. Once at the railing however, we were stopped and had to wait for two hours before being let off the ship. Apparently there was a union strike of dock workers and alternate help had to be found.

Finally we were back in the arms of Thelma who had a party waiting for us. We knew none of the people but were warmly received. All expressed concern for us, not only because of the cyclone but for our being in the hands of the communists for eighteen days! They soon found we had enjoyed the trip and were none the worse. The captain, at the end of the trip, had invited us to come visit him and his wife at their dacha outside Moscow. We could not have been more warmly received by all the Russians we met.

Some five years latter a newspaper article reported that the Mickhail Lermintov sank in the straights off New Zeland. Its new Captain would not allow anyone to board the ship to help with evacuation. The newspaper reported speculation that it was full of spy equipment they didn't want discovered. Regretably two sailors lost their lives. Of course Bob's beautiful painting, no doubt, went down with the ship. Captain Borodin had told us it would be retired with the ship and placed in the permanent collection of the Russian Maritime Museum in Moscow.

On the last leg of our trip Thelma took us for a drive to the Montclair Baptist Church in New Jersey where Bob had worked with Fred Lamb. I was awed by the murals he painted there and thrilled to get to see these works of his youth. His minature door to the childrens' classroom was a delight and looked as if it had been planned and placed there as part of the original building. However happy we were, we were weary travelers and ready to head for home.

Chapter 42

Bob's oldest daughter Hannah called welcoming us home and said she hoped to see us soon perhaps at their home in Florida. Bob was excited to hear from her. He very much loved and missed seeing his older daughter more often. She was a realtor in Florida and her business and family occupied her time. Her father was very proud of her business success.

When spring came we were in Florida on Bob's birthday. More precisely we were out on a fishing boat in the Gulf of Mexico with Bob wrestling the biggest fish the captain said his vessel had ever hauled in! It took three men to help pull it to the side then, with a snare, hoist it aboard. As an inlander, I had never seen such a big fish! It looked like a monster when first breaking out of the water. It had a gigantic head, huge eyes and mouth. It was a grupper weighing, by a guess-as we never found out beyond a guess-maybe over a hundred pounds! All on board were jubilant. Hannah and I embraced and hugged each other then the "man of the hour." Rather spent from the struggle, he hardly knew what to make of his good fortune and birthday gift. It filled our freezer when filleted, iced, and shipped back to Williamsburg.

This event was occasioned by an invitation from Bob's daughter, Hannah, living in the panhandle of Florida on the Gulf of Mexico. Having fully recovered from our Russian trip of the previous summer, we flew down braving a transfer at the labyrinth of Atlanta airport.

Hannah had taken time out from her very busy and successful real estate business to give us attention. When we first arrived she had a birthday party all prepared and held on their patio looking out over the water. We were delighted to see shrimp boats passing by while we ate. This was apparently unusual. Bob was feeling good and in his element with a whole party of people and him as guest of honor! He was never short of stories and humor, and kept Hannah's party lively. We were early risers and the next mornings fishing expedition was no strain after our night of revelry.

We enjoyed visiting with Hannah and her husband Russell. Bob was especially fond of Russell, as a son he never had. Unfortunately there would be few visits after this. Hannah kept in touch but came to Williamsburg infrequently in subsequent years. Sadly she would die of lung cancer just a few months after her father's death some years later. Wishing to spare her father and confident she would outlive him, she had not let us know she had cancer. Bob loved his family and many made trips to Neck-O-Land Road during our marriage.

The great grandchildren came and spent several weeks in the summers. One great grandson spent an extended period of time with us, after a breakup in his family. We had wanted him to stay permanently but he had come from Glouster and a fishing environment and wanted to go to his grandmother, Hannah, in Florida. He wanted to live where there was "big time fishing," he said. He would grow up to marry a fishingboat captain's daughter!

With Bush Garden, Colonial Williamsburg, and motel swimming pools, as well as the public library, there was always plenty for the children to do. I escourted them to these places. Bob had lost his interest in magic shows, ferris-wheels, roller coaster rides, and wild animal shows. Though the children tried persuading me, I drew the line when it came to the roller coaster ride. No amount of persuasion could lure me to so reckless an adventure--at my age.

Before we left and Bob had dolled out spending money, he held the children for a bit of lighthearted lecturing, on the benefits of frugality, before they could leave. The youngsters sighed, shifted feet, and patiently listened until finally being freed. They then dashed to the car where I was already waiting. They loved their grandfather and endulged his old fashioned ways. I had some of my own ways they were less ready to accept-- without complaint. However, I stuck to what I knew was best for them--the teacher was still in me--and I was responsible for them.

Bob handled his own money in a strange manner as seen in the use of his bank security deposit box. He rented a box but put next to nothing in it, though he visited it regularly. Sometimes he would carry an envelope with small bills to deposit. He would dress in his finest suit and tie for this trip to the bank! He polished his shoes and 'wore' his fanciest cane with a carved handle! Like John Ringling. he projected himself as king of his domain.   One could speculate that he did this to make an impression on the employees and everyone there at the bank! He was ever mindful of the image of wealth he wanted to project in this small community of Williamsburg.

Believing John Ringling when he said,"People respect you more when you act like you have money," he certainly looked like a million dollars when he made this monthly trip to the bank! The reality was that Bob kept what money he had in a chimney at home! It was not exorbitant but was enough to make moderate loans to people, if asked. However, he never spoke to me of being asked; though he did relate that this was something he did. He said he loaned to people without interest and they always paid him back.

Some years later a local merchant came to me after dark one evening and in an emotional appeal expressed his immediate need for money. He said he had been referred by a good friend of my late husband and was in need of several thousand dollars to meet payment of a shipment coming in the next day-a Friday. He said he had already made several big sales but would be paid only when the parties received their goods. He would return the money to me the next day! I wondered who the referral had come from? The merchant would not tell me.

Chapter 43

In the early days of our marriage guests were never ending and the parking lot always had a strange car in it. Both our families and friends came frequently. Those from out of town sometimes stayed for several days. They usually wanted to see Colonial Williamsburg as well as us. After the much visiting, and meeting the new person, summer went into fall and we, more or less, had Webb's Acre to ourselves. It was time to think of starting a project.

Bob wanted another rental house and it seemed reasonable to have one. We did a lot of calculating and determined that it would pay for itself, in rents, in a few years. I suggested that I make this my project and Bob agreed. It would be built back by the woods and called the Wheel House. Bob said, "Go ahead with it. It's yours!" I called on my college architectural drawing experience and made several sketches of a small cottage. The floor plan and elevation were added and with a minor change by the "master builder," Bob Webb, the plans were submitted to the County Planning Office. They were approved and we hammered the building permit to a tree by the driveway.

Men came out and poured a cement slab and carpenters proceeded to frame up the walls. We had planned on doing the interior ourselves and took over when the framing and electrical work was completed. We worked on insulating walls, installed counter-tops, sinks, a shower, and did many other things to complete the Wheel House. Working together and with me learning from Bob, we got the fourth rental cottage finished.

Women today make their living doing such things. In the 1980's it was still, more or less, a novelty. This was something I wanted to do, though it would be a once in a lifetime project, thus perhaps a waste of learning. I told myself, however, that many things of worth are done only once. It was our project and we had pride in doing it together and completing it while remaining lovers and friends!

At various times inspectors came out and

approved the electrical, plumbing, and other work. Finally completed, we painted the large iron wagon wheel by the Barn door and rolled it up the driveway standing it on the side of the Wheel House. The Barn still had its horse collar. Our first tenant was thrilled to find this place as he had lived in a real wheel house on a boat and said he felt right at home here!

Projects were what defined the seasons for us. No matter what time of year it was, we needed to be busy and involved. After several years of 'doing' including the raising of our dog Tippy from a handful of fluff we adopted from the SPCA, we took stock of what we could do next. Bob envisioned a split-rail fence around the whole property and we discused the merits of it. Such a fence would primarily be for looks as it would keep nothing out from the woods, nor would it keep in the dog and any future chickens. He still liked the idea and called in the Indian carpenter, Clyde, to do the work. Finished, the fence had a rustic, rural look and enclosed the whole property accept for the front driveway entrance.

It truly did enhance the property. However, some years later I was surprised to look out the kitchen window and see two cows standing in my garden in the back! Bob said they didn't jump the fence to get there. They probably sauntered up Neck-O-Land Road and turned into the driveway going all the way to the back garden! We called the dairy farmer and he came and got his property, ushering them down the drive and down the road to home.

Next I asked Bob if he didn't want chickens and a garden? I teased him that I had planned to marry a farmer and thought I had! A very important activity for me was gardening. When single I had rented a garden plot from the city, as many other city dwellers did, from one large acreage divided up. I knew the thrill of seeing things grow. Bob said that from the time he had first started developing Webb's Acre, he had wanted these things. He was delighted that I shared his interest and decided it was time the dream came true. We would have a garden and chickens.

A carpenter friend from Colonial Williamsburg was called to convert the shed to a chicken coop. Bobs' right hand man, Shorty, was instructed to turn the ground over, back by the woods, for a garden. There had been a plot there years earlier tended by Shorty. It had lain dormant for many years. In retrospect I did enjoy gardening but have to credit our gardener for much of the weeding. He still came and tended the grounds and I'm sure when I was occupied elsewhere he weeded.

We shared both vegetables and our chickens with Shorty. When the hens got too old to lay eggs he would bind up their legs and carry them home, alive, on the city bus.

Our Rhode Island Red hens were easy to care for and the big brown eggs they laid were a wonderful addition to our table. Bob enjoyed making adjustments to their nesting boxes, perches and feeding troughs. When owls threatened, and killed one hen, he closed in their yard space behind the shed and put chicken wire over the top, thus solving the problem. If we wanted to go away for a weekend, usually to the mountains, a neighbor or one of the tenants was always willing to feed and water the hens as well as care for our dog, Tippy.

We loved the Blue Ridge Mountains where Bob liked to do small, what he called pocket paintings, later to become larger works at his easel back home. The mountains were about a three hour drive from our home. We would spend a weekend in a motel or lodge and take walks out into the countryside where Bob would set up his outdoor easel and folding chair and paint. I usually brought a book along or a sketchpad. These memories, as paintings, now hang on my wall.

Chapter 44

A memorable trip, that wasn't a trip, happened in the late fall. We decided to take one last weekend and stay in a particular lodge we liked just off the Skyline Drive. We asked a tenant to take care of the chickens and gather the eggs each day. He would also feed Tippy and spend time playing ball with her--a toss and fetch game she loved.

As a border collie she couldn't get enough running and would often take off running up and down the drive and around in circles in the yard just for the fun of it. She always knew when we were going away and, not liking it, would disappear into her doghouse and just stay there. She didn't like our leaving her but, on the other hand, she didn't like going with us either.

All packed and ready we were still late in getting started, having taken time to instruct the tenant on how to retrieve an egg from a sitting hen ! The lodge we were going to had a pleasant dinningroom and comfortable lounge areas with burning gaslog fireplaces. One wall of window looked out over the Appalachian valley and a beautiful lake. This time of year there would still be colorful trees and deep blue sky and crystal clear water.

I was driving and our late start only brought us to the foothills, when dusk settled down around us. Darkness would soon follow. Needing gasoline I turned into the first service station, which was probably the last before entering the parkway drive. I pulled up to the punp and Bob got out and filled the tank. He leaned into the window and gestured for me to look at the old truck parked over to the side.

It reminded us of the 1930's when homeless people traveled with everything they owned piled high on their trucks. It listed to one side as if in danger of sliding over, or about to give a last gasp and collapse. Loaded down and piled high with old furniture-a table, chairs, bar stool, a treadle sewing machine, lamps sticking out at all angles, it had dozens of cardboard boxes disintegrating from past rains and winds. All was topped off with two mattresses that had constantly bumped against a broken mirror and now spewed puffs of stuffing into the air! Another mile and the whole load would have been scattered on the highway.

Bob paid for the gasoline and asked me to pull over and park by the truck. A boney young man of indistinguished origin and ragged clothing was tugging at his cargo as if to rearrange it for a better fit. Bob had opened our car trunk and pulled out a very long heavy rope. It had been there for years just waiting for this day and occasion! Bob walked up to the fellow and asked if he could help. He then handed Toby-that may not have been his name- the rope telling him to hang on to one end and throw the rest over the top of the mattresses. Bob went around and caught it and tied it down on a rail along the side. He went to the other side, where the young man stood, and instructed him in tying that end down. With yet twice as much rope left, they made two more passes over the top and firmly tied them.

I had looked in the cab of the truck and could see a frail young woman and her two girls about six and eight who were poorly dressed in flimsy summer dresses. They were shivering. It had turned quite cold. While the men worked I took a blanket we had always kept in the car and walked over to the open window (if it had a window), and asked the mother if she would take it for the girls to wrap themselves in. I said I wanted to give it to them and they could keep it. She very gratefully accepted and tucked it around their shoulders, while thanking me.

Bob talked with the fellow and learned he had come up from Texas and was on his way to a job in New Jersey.

They had not eaten for some time nor had they stopped and rested anywhere. They didn't know the north would be so cold; or their trip so long. They had no winter clothes and no money until the first paycheck of the new job he was going to.

I was again in the car thinking of how these people reminded me of the Picasso blue period painting called "At the Waters Edge." I remembered seeing it every day as I went to classes held in The Art Institute of Chicago. It caused me to shiver then! They reminded Bob of his early days during the great depression when his own two young girls needed winter clothes. Sitting here in our gift of a fancy Chrysler New Yorker, I wondered what kind of weekend we would have? The weather was cold and the higher we would go in the mountains the colder it would get. Most of the beautiful leaves were already gone. Bob wouldn't want to sit outside and paint nor would we want to stay in beside a fireplace no more cozy than our own at home.

Just then Bob leaned back through the window and said, "I think Tippy is missing us. What do you say I give them the $100 dollars we were going to spend this weekend and go home?" This was before the days of credit cards and we could not have gone on to the lodge. It was also when $100 would pay for a weekend and food in a mountain lodge ! We never carried a check book and if we had, it still seemed a better idea to go home. "My thoughts exactly." I answered. The young man wanted our address, that he might repay us, but Bob told him to just help someone someday if he saw them in need.

Toby's angels left him there and headed back where they came from. They were pleased with what they had done and drove along with jubilant pleasure knowing they had helped this young family. They also shared their own thanksgiving for living through and surviving the hard times of the great depression of the 1930s. They both had memories of deprivation and struggles during those years of their childhood and youth. They had both persevered.

When arriving home, Tippy was out of her doghouse leaping and frolicing with joy! The tenant was equally happy to see us as he confided his fear of the next morning and being pecked by the hens! I said I would be happy as well if I didn't have to cook tonight. After all we had planned to have a nice meal at a mountain lodge dinningroom. We changed the location and kept the name by going to the Lodge dining room at Colonial Williamsburg. that evening ! It had very fine cuisine.

Finally, at days end, it was good to be home and relaxing before our own roaring fire, from gas logs we had already installed some time ago. If we had planned it, we couldn't have planned a better trip with any happier outcome. We went to bed thinking of that young couple. We knew they would survive and this would be a memory for them.

Chapter 45

$\mathcal{B}$ ob finally became the mentor he wanted to be. I wanted to add painting conservation to my art experiences and he was eager to teach me. He was not always an easy teacher. He had the view that learning was earning! As a boy he was frequently required to do manual labor before his mentor would tell him something.! He didn't mean for me to go out and chop wood before he would tell me a particular procedure but I had to earn my way! I was to learn one step well before going on to the next. We had been practicing on old oil paintings from where ever we could find them.

The most important bit of instruction was that I have a notebook and begin to copy down everything Bob did. I was to note the time it took for a procedure, solvents used, steps involved, drying times, and on and on. I simply watched him and kept a written record of all that he did and all that he used. The time came for me to work with him. He turned out to be a good teacher with infinate patience ! Bob's patience always amazed me ! I could make the dumbest, most crucial mistakes and he never reprimanded or even gave me a look of disgust. He quietly corrected me or said nothing. With other people, in other circumstances he could be volatile. Years latter my notebook came in handy more than once when I got stuck on a procedure and needed to know something. It was there in my notebook.

We allowed perhaps two or three years for this work, serving mostly the community of Williamsburg. Not wanting to feel burdened by being scheduled to meet deadlines, we took in only what paintings we wanted to complete in a short period of time. After my learning and a few restoration jobs, we did no more work and I didn't pick it up again until some years later. Now, in my senoir years, it has proved to be an enjoyable vocation.

As a change of pace and loving baroque music for the harpsichord, I wanted to play this instrument that had such a lovely sound. I asked Bob if we might find a used harpsichord somewhere; maybe the Music Man at C.W. would know of one. My dear husband who was always sure I could do anything, said he thought rather that I could make one if I really wanted it! His confidence made me believe I could! After a little research, we ordered a Zuckerman English Bentside Spinet Harpsicord kit and I went to work in the garage. First however, I nearly lost my courage after reading the two inch thick manual of instructions ! After that one moment of panic however, I just took a deep breath and got started.

At five a.m. each morning with coffee mug in hand, I crossed the drive to the garage to spend three hours of concentrated work. At eight a.m. and back in the house my regular day's routine was started by preparing breakfast. Those six weeks of early morning hours in April were beautiful and I came to love the balm in the air and first blush of dawn with chirping of waking birds. The garage became my sanctified workplace.

With dry weather all the time, this spinet harpsichord was completed, without a hitch, in six weeks. It stood seven feet long and three and a half feet tall with the top closed. With the top open and light reflecting off the brass strings and polished soundboard, I thought it was beautiful!

I asked Bob to put the finish on it as he was a master at this and I knew he could do a better job than I could. It was a joy to watch him work using long even brush strokes giving a professional finish to our baby- grand -style ancient musical instrument. After it was dry in two days and we were carrying it up the back steps and into the house the first rain drops came. I looked to the heavens and said, "thanks." Rain, at anytime in this garage construction period, would have warped the wood and ruined it.

The C.W. music man came out to see it and play it. To hear it being played by a professional was a thrill. He said I had done a fine job. The tone indicated a correct shaving of the soundboard. The wires were wound tightly around the pegs and the qwills were precision spaced. Bob was proud of my work. His pride meant much to me knowing what a fine craftsman he was himself. He would point out to everyone who came to the house what I had done! I think friends and family and even I, grew weary of his excess of exuberance. However, I loved him for it, knowing how important his morale support had been.

Bob never came to the garage during my 5:00a.m. to 8:00a.m. schedule of working. He had an interest each evening as I studied the manual for the next days work. I then left the manual in the house remembering what was expected for the next day. I appreciated that Bob left me alone to realize the limit of what I could do. It was, without a doubt the most difficult yet most satisfying project I'ed ever taken on.We enjoyed our harpsichord although it constantly needed tuning due to the dampness where we lived. Years latter, now widowed, I sold it to a collector of ancient musical instruments who wanted it for his museum in New York! I was gratified to know it would be taken care of and have a museum home. It didn't bother me that he mistakenly thought it was Bob, the master builder from Colonial Williamsburg, who had built it! I had not advertised it as such and saw no reason to correct him. He played it and examined it's every detail. I had painted my name deep inside the enclosed case. Perhaps a hundred years from now some restorer will find it and credit it's construction to a 20th century woman craftsman.

Chapter 46

We both liked to dress in our finery and go out to dinner at least once a week. I had just finished sewing an outfit for myself and Bob had gone to a tailor to be fitted for a new suit. As he had planned, it was ready on our wedding anniversary! That evening, feeling very spiffy indeed, we went back to the Williamsburg Inn to celebrate our tenth year together.

Sometimes we would go to church then go out to eat. We would go to Bob's preference, the Christian Science Church. One particular morning I could see something was on Bob's mind and he couldn't, or didn't want to talk about it. That day we went to one of Williamsburgs fine restaurants that had a quiet atmosphere.

Bob reached across the table and took my

hand; then he finally told me what was bothering him. He said he knew his time was getting short and he didn't want to leave me! Such reflection drained me but we both knew this would come some day. The public location, here in a resturant, kept me from crying. We had anticipated this but didn't know how to meet it. Bob had always been anxious about death and could not be consoled. He loved life so much. I thought a doctor's opinion might help but the suggestion was met by scorn. He couldn't be persuaded to see a doctor until his misery became great enough. Then he went to have his heart checked. Afterward he only scoffed at the test results saying that everybody dies of the same thing anyway, their heart stops beating!

With each day, small distractions were events that called for attention and gave meaning to our lives. Whether this was Tippy needing a bath-we had a deep sink in the garage in which she just fit-or me fitting a new suit to my dress form and then sewing it, Bob sat with chin on his cane, intently observing. We made rounds visiting friends-some of whom were in the hospital. We had some friends we traded dinners with in each other's homes.

Sometimes the men did the cooking! Bob had an English retired army officer friend who liked certain English dishes. Bob would reciprocate with his own favorite English specialty meals. We thus kept active or were passively busy most of the time. It's hard to change one's pattern of a lifetime.

One of Bobs 'passive busy' thinking periods led to another building project ! This would be the last building project and was something he very much wanted. In no way could I discourage it. That would be the addition of a front porch to the main house. Bob wanted a screened porch to "just sit on and enjoy the front yard and nature" he said. He did the measuring and drew up the plans for it but took no part in the actual building. Rather, he called in Clyd, his Native American carpenter, who did a good job constructing a hurricane proof screened porch. Bob enjoyed just sitting on a chair and watching him work. At this time in his life he enjoyed just watching others work.

We furnished the porch modestly and enjoyed many afternoons there talking, having tea, and napping.

For one final addition we went shopping and picked out a young tree to plant at the end of the porch ! Shorty dug the hole far enough out for a very large tree to have room to branch. This is something Bob wanted and after planting it got some teasing from his friends that he would never live to see it grow. They had missed the point he said.

The huge fireplace was a great pleasure where we spent evenings listening to our favorite music or just sitting quietly watching the fire. Our gas logs were a joy. What a blessing for older people who can't, or don't want to carry logs from outdoors. We enjoyed classical and some popular music and had special pieces that just seemed to belong to us. Occasionally we danced together in the living room ! Bob never lost his playfulness and if I was busy in the kitchen, he would pick up my dress form from the foyer and, holding out a jacket arm drapped over it, he would waltz to the kitchen. I would trade places with the mannequin to dance with him, leaving the dishes for later. Relaxing by the fireplace, Bob told stories of his childhood or the people he knew. He told of the many varied jobs he had been commissioned to do. His stories were enough to fill a book.

Chapter 47

The back patio was a favorite spot for just sitting and watching the birds. Various species of birds flew in and out of their houses Bob had built and hung on the garage, the smokehouse, and the barn when these structures first went up. Also, bluejays claimed the front yard and cardinals a big tree in the back. Mockingbirds had a nest each year above the climbing rose bush over the dinning room window. After many years of work, being scheduled, and committed to one project or another, this was relaxing. Life was good and it seemed it should never end. But it did. Time ran out.

His heart gave out and after a short illness Bob died July 11, 1987 at home on his beloved Webb's Acre.

True to his wish Bob died with very little money left. He expressed his feeling that a life, well lived, would not have stored wealth at the end. During his lifetime he had provided for those he loved. He had succeeded, as he wished, in projecting an image of wealth to some. He might have been a wealthy man, and at times perhaps he was, however he chose not to leave wealth. He had everything he wanted, though his wants were modest.

Bob gave lavishly in life, to his family, friends, and strangers. For a long time, as a never ending stream, he was always able to give! As a tribute while he lived, his neighbor, the professor, observed that, "Bob Webb had exceptional intellegence and talent and could have been anything he wanted to be in life." He then paused and added, "but you know, Bob was exactly what he wanted to be." He left grand memories, his effusive nature was both big and decisive, generous yet frugal. He loved his nation and his family. He was a perfectionist yet forgiving of imperfection. He was lovable and loving.

Robert James Webb, Jr. has left a legacy in his art works, long to be remembered from Massachusetts, New Jersey, New York, North Carolina, Florida, and Williamsburg, Virginia. In historic places, mansions, libraries, churches,

and many public places where his art played a
part, Robert Webb, though he never signed his
work, has left his signature in color, form, and
beauty.